Rhymes
of the
Times

Poems from 2020 and Beyond

ED RIEDERICH

WESTBOW
PRESS®
A DIVISION OF THOMAS NELSON
& ZONDERVAN

WestBow Press books may be ordered through booksellers or by contacting:

WestBow Press
A Division of Thomas Nelson & Zondervan
1663 Liberty Drive
Bloomington, IN 47403
www.westbowpress.com
844-714-3454

ISBN: 978-1-6642-6656-8 (sc)
ISBN: 978-1-6642-6655-1 (hc)
ISBN: 978-1-6642-6657-5 (e)

Library of Congress Control Number: 2022908797

Print information available on the last page.

WestBow Press rev. date: 05/21/2022

Contents

To my amazing high school English teacher, Claire Teague. She inspired me to write poetry thirty years ago, and she continues to inspire me today.

Foreword

Think of the wisest person you know. How has that person impacted you? Do you look up to them? Do you know them on a personal level? Thankfully, I have been blessed to know my wisest person on one of the most personal levels possible. He is my father. My father's character is one of wisdom, integrity, and discipline, but I would be a fool to think he has become those things through his own strength. He has wisdom and gifts because he consistently and fervently runs to the source of true wisdom, Jesus Christ. Jesus has always been the center focus of my father's life. I have witnessed firsthand the fruit in his life with his generosity, genuine care for others, the way he treats my mother, and so much more. He has always understood that apart from the vine, the branches are worth nothing. He has tenaciously applied this principal to his life for as long as I can remember.

God has shown him what to write about many times. He has spoken to both himself and to others through his poetry. This book is important because it's full of wisdom, something we are experiencing a drought of. I'm not talking about a worldly wisdom founded upon vain knowledge. I'm talking about profound, godly wisdom that can only come from the Most High. We are thirsty for truth and hope, especially with the state of the world now. We must begin seeking God's presence with fervor and desperation or such a drought will persist. My father's poetry is a roaring river amidst this parched desert, pressing us on to seek God's presence. His poetry is full of godly wisdom written by a man who spends time in prayer and loves the Lord.

Reading my dad's poetry leaves me feeling deeply inspired, spiritually nourished, and voraciously hungry for more. That is why I am writing this. I want you to experience what I have had the privilege to experience for so long. Open your heart and mind, and enjoy the brilliant gift God has given to my father, the wisest person I know. His poetry will bless you like it has blessed me.

—Katelyn Riederich

Give Me Liberty

*Nathan Hale said, "I only regret that I have
but one life to lose for my country."*

Give me liberty, or give me death!
I will fight to the last breath!
But something changed in this liberty cry;
I realized I really did not want to die.

Give me liberty, but let someone else fight.
Let someone else preserve my liberty right.
I will root them on and give them my support.
Give me liberty while I hide in my fort.

Thoughts entered: *Is freedom outdated?*
Has liberty become truly overrated?
Give me liberty, but don't hold your breath.
I want liberty, but I don't want death.

Give me liberty, but I want security more.
I lay all my rights down on the floor.
I will take false peace over my liberty.
I'm tired of all this negativity.

OK, my liberty is now for sale.
What was wrong with Nathan Hale?
Forget liberty; just give me peace.
From this struggle, I need released.

I sold my liberty, and all was lost.
Not realizing liberty came at a cost,
I traded my liberty for security,
Choosing to be silent and live in obscurity.

Goodbye, liberty; men came and took.
Now only remembered in history books,
Liberty's plan has gone askew.
Left with no liberty, only a statue.

Poets of the Modern Day

Who are the poets of the modern day?
Eloquent words but nothing to say.
On the balance, little to weigh.

Who are the songwriters of the modern day?
A catchy tune but nothing to say.
Will be forgotten soon, though now they play.

Corruption into words they weave,
Deceiving the minds of the naïve.
Shallow messages for you to believe.

Modern poetry I'm not adoring.
Words with wings but are not soaring.
Truthfully, most of it is boring.

Another poem that doesn't rhyme.
Another waste of my time.
Poetic stanzas not worth a dime.

These poems can be read from universities,
About social injustice and diversity.
I'd rather hear about triumph through adversity.

Fancy words that don't stick,
Like sweet-smelling candles so thick
But with no fire on their wick.

I listen closely in the walls of the poetic
To hear some truth or the prophetic,
Yet all I hear is the voice of the pathetic.

Is there a poet? Is there a voice?
To hear the truth, I would rejoice.
Modern poets must make their choice.

Many please others out of fear.
So truth hides and lies come near,
Speaking what itching ears want to hear.

Give us a poet and a songwriter.
For the truth, give us a fighter.
Give us candle, but give us a lighter.

The Valley We Descend

(In response to the poem "The Hill We Climb," recited at the Presidential Inauguration on January 20, 2021)

Through the hourglass of time rang out the words: "the hill we climb." Those words to the forefront did ascend. And to those words, my ears did bend.

Words to our nation, yet a shallow sound, not breaking up any fallow ground.
Give the writer a pen, and they will write. But with their words, can they give us sight?

In perilous times, we need more than the poetic. We need a message of substance, something prophetic
For a while, "The Hill We Climb" did trend, but now hear my words: "the valley we descend."

A border crisis, inflation, and taxes. At the trees of justice are laid the axes. Blaming others couldn't be any dumber. Too many playing the victim, too few overcomers.

Murder and violence in our cities, and for the child in the womb no pity Evil is called good, and good is called evil. And all around us unrest and upheaval.

The sky is blackened as we descend. Can we now our ways amend? Righteousness we cannot pretend. Truth and liberty we must defend.

So the flag goes dark as we descend, but yet the flag, we still must extend. The road of humility we will walk, not giving heed to the voices that mock.

The valley will be long, and it will be hard. But our covenant with God we must guard.
Our nation has walked valleys before. We've gone through hardships. We've gone through war.

A place of darkness and division moving into a valley of decision.
May we continue a little longer. The dark valley will make us stronger.

Our republic travels into this ravine, a place our country has never seen. New trials we haven't experienced before, but we must remember Psalm 23:4.

In this darkness, we hear wicked voices, but we will be measured by each of our choices.
As you read these words, let it sink in. Today will we find a modern-day Lincoln?

The sands of the hourglass continue to fall. America's valley, America's call. Enough from the elitists and the haters. We must turn back to our Creator.

And in our grain of hourglass sand, for God and liberty may we stand.
For America's future, we must contend through the valley we now descend.

The Necessity of Wind

The Biosphere 2 project was created as a research tool for scientists to study earth's living systems. From 1991 to 1993, eight volunteers sealed themselves from the outside world in this bubble. It is remembered as a failure. In the Biosphere 2, trees grew faster than they would have in the wild. However, they found that these trees couldn't completely mature. Before they could, they would collapse. Later, it was found that this was caused by a lack of wind in the biosphere. The presence of wind makes a tree stronger. The tree is then able to mature and not fall down due to its own weight.

Biosphere 2
An enclosed region
Tried to recreate
The Garden of Eden

Trees grew quick
But never matured
A failed experiment
That never endured

Weak trees enclosed
Leaves had thinned
Trees with no strength
Because they had no wind

Protected in a bubble
Brought an end not good
Beautiful but not strong
Developed no stress wood

We deal with contrary winds
Adversity that seems wrong
But don't forget its purpose
The purpose to make you strong

At Biosphere 2
In all their pursuits
They had beautiful trees
Yet with shallow roots

We go through valleys
We go through trials
Some can be long
And go on for miles

But roots are developed
When the wind blows
Through those blistering gusts
The weak tree grows

Making you stronger
Is God's master plan
And in that wind
Is where strength began

Raising Cain

There once was a man named Cain,
And to the earth he came.
To do what was right, he was able,
But he sat alone at his table.
Half-hearted sacrifice a stain.

To do right, he did not yield,
But killed Abel in the field,
Rejecting the word of correction.
A vagabond with no direction,
His fate became sealed.

Now look at our youth today.
This generation has lost its way.
Who are the ones now raising Cain?
At whose feet do we lay the blame?
No black and white, only gray.

Is it professors? Is it teachers?
Is it parents? Is it preachers?
Parents who don't show the way.
Preachers with soft sermons today.
No responsibility they feature.

Always passing, never failing.
Through life, only smooth sailing.
Never learning from defeat,
So bad habits they do repeat.
In living right, not prevailing.

Through our land, you will see Cains
Calling out for violence and pain.
We have kicked out God everywhere.
In our schools, kicked out prayer.
Now there is hate in their veins.

Are we able to see the insane?
Can we feel God's heart and pain?
In our homes and at our tables,
Are we able to raise up an Abel
While others keep on raising Cain?

Frog in the Boiling Pot

From the frog's point of view, and with the help of my daughter Katelyn.

Stay at home.
It helps a lot.
So I jump inside
The cold-water pot.

And while in the pot,
Can you wear a mask?
It helps, you know.
Not much we ask.

The water gets warmer,
But doing what I should.
We're all in this together
For the greater good.

Starting now to sweat.
Do I have a fever?
Is this the virus?
I think I'm a believer.

I stay in the water
As the lid covers the pot.
I do not question it.
The greater good I've sought.

As the lid clangs down,
My freedom is lost.
Not questioning the hand
Comes at a great cost.

Darkness surrounds me.
Confined and restricted,
Becoming harder to breathe,
Feeling more constricted.

What is this I see?
As the bubbles surround,
Now I am sweating.
Water all around.

Now in a rolling boil,
Freedom croaked in this pot.
It may be too late for me,
But for you it's not.

Saved from the Auschwitz Train

In a small Belarusian village, the Nazis came to take Jewish families to Auschwitz. On the way, a brave mother threw her ten-year-old daughter over the neighbor's fence. A soldier saw it, but he pretended he did not. The girl survived a freezing cold night in the neighbor's barn. She faced many difficulties, from hiding to orphanages. She went through many hardships, but Jesus was with her through it all. The mother took a step of courage that saved her daughter's life.

There was a brave mother of Belarus
Soldiers came in times so tense
The grip on her child's hand was loose
She threw her girl over the neighbor's fence

A Nazi soldier saw it with his own eyes
But he ignored the action in her defense
To her mother there were no goodbyes
But she survived this moment so intense

Through the struggles and desperate cries
Trials and tests she could not understand
What God meant for good was in disguise
He had her in the palm of His hand

What she went through I cannot begin to explain
But her brave mother saved her from the Auschwitz train

Eggs Benedict

Tainted eggs were laid years ago.
Now we reap what's been sown.
Infected eggs we did not catch.
Glance around and see them hatch.

Liberal hens have laid these eggs,
Striving to give communism legs.
Look through the common-sense lens.
There's something wrong with these hens.

Isn't there someone who truly sees?
These chicks have a deadly disease.
In colleges, these chicks are celebrated.
Youth not knowing they are contaminated.

I'm saddened by our schools.
History taught by many fools.
Harvesting chicks for a reason,
Pushing their agenda of treason.

Those who question are labeled as haters,
Yet so many cannot see these traitors.
Is anyone among us startled?
Look and you can see Benedict Arnold.

Benedicts in our government.
For evil, they do not relent.
Benedicts seen in big tech.
Restrictions with no benefit.

Every mandate they use to restrict
Shows the preparing of Eggs Benedict.

Skippy the Squirrel

The other day, I stepped outside
I said, "Wow, it's nippy."
Then I heard a voice say,
"Actually, my name is Skippy."

I scanned my backyard.
I looked here and there.
I looked down and saw this squirrel.
He was sitting in a chair.

He sat there, reading a paper.
He had his legs crossed.
I thought this squirrel is crazy.
On the ground, there's frost.

I said, "Nice to meet you, Skippy."
He peered over his glasses.
He said, "Look at our media.
They've deceived the masses."

I said, "I know what you mean.
I agree with you, Skippy.
It's like Chinese water torture—
A drip machine so drippy."

His glasses' arm was in his mouth.
The news he didn't want to discuss.
But then he pointed at the paper
And said, "Our leaders are just nuts."

I know a few things about nuts.
I know an acorn from a pistachio.
But I definitely didn't know more
Than this squirrel on my patio.

I said, "I know about their agenda,
And believe me, it's really trippy.
They don't care about the people
Or even squirrels like you, Skippy."

He said, "We store up for winter,
Then they take our provision.
They speak of compassion,
But then they cause division.

"And what I have stored up,
They distribute to others.
Then they tax me on what's left
So they can give it to another.

"It makes us squirrels angry.
I want to rise in defiance.
They want to force us to obey
And say we can't question science.

"They've covered their ears.
They don't listen to critiques.
I shake my head in my chair,
Sitting on my squirrel cheeks."

Skippy said, "Now look, I gotta go.
I'm meeting a chipmunk named Scottie.
We work out every Thursday,
And we do yoga and Pilates."

"No problem, sir, at all.
I'm still a little nippy.
But I'm glad to meet you,
And stay strong, Skippy."

I watched him run up a tree
Before his yoga classes.
I thought, *I sure learned a lot
From a squirrel in glasses.*

Bird in the Cage

Don't be the bird in the cage,
Staring at the open door with your eyes.
Go through the curtain on the stage.

To fly, the risk you can gauge,
But risk or not, you must fly.
Don't be the bird in the cage.

Don't be hindered because of your age.
Into fear, you must not buy.
Go through the curtain on the stage.

Yes, men will hate, and fools will rage.
You can't waste your time asking why.
Don't be the bird in the cage.

To the next chapter, turn the page.
Sadly, some never do and then die.
Go through the curtain on the stage.

Your calling is more than a wage.
You were predestined to soar high.
Don't be the bird in the cage.
Go through the curtain on the stage.

Boy Meets Girl

Boy meets girl,
But girl becomes man.
Boy is confused.
He doesn't understand.

So boy becomes girl,
As girl becomes man.
Is everyone confused
By the natural plan?

As girl becomes man,
The man becomes neutral.
What does that mean?
That sounds unfruitful.

And man who became girl
Now identifies as a flower.
It doesn't smell sweet,
But I guess she feels power.

Girl who became neutral
Now identifies as a train.
In all their identifying,
They have lost their brain.

In their foundation,
I see huge cracks.
This runaway train
Has gone off the tracks.

See, there was Adam,
And there was Eve.
Eve didn't change
And become Steve.

And in that garden,
With that man Adam,
He didn't change
And become a madam.

I will try to be sensitive.
I will try to be gentle.
But when they swap what's natural,
They have then become mental.

America in the Balance

Help me to see, Land of Liberty,
America's written story.
Men have trod with help from God,
Faithful for old glory.

Through the flood, men spilled their blood,
Though sinking in the mire.
Through every war, shaken to the core,
We walked right through the fire.

Forgotten our Maker, freedom takers
Silencing our free speech.
Unbalanced measure succumb to pressure,
Pandering to every leech.

I think of the past. How long will we last?
That is a haunting mystery.
Led now by fools, brainwashed schools
Erasing our history.

Is any hearing to be God fearing?
Time will only tell.
This hour demands that we must stand.
The truth we must not sell.

Through the tests, God's word suggests
His Spirit will be our water.
To fear don't give way, but only pray
For our sons and daughters.

In this hour, we need God's power.
We cannot live to please us.
For our survival, we need a revival
And a turning back to Jesus.

Heroes of Flight 93

Written on September 11, 2021.

Passengers aboard flight 93,
Heroes they will always be.
Yet these heroes we do not see.

Ordinary people like you and me,
They would not go down silently,
Etched in our hearts permanently.

With terrorists, they did not plea.
They stood up with no guarantee,
Knowing then freedom isn't free.

An act of bravery we can all agree.
In that moment, they could not foresee
How much they would inspire you and me.

Have we forgotten flight 93?
Those scattered in a field of debris,
Heroes to me, they will always be.

Aunt Ifa

There once was a woman named Aunt Ifa.
She was seen from Portland to Topeka.
For every city, she had a surprise,
And she had a fire in her eyes.
See her in Seattle or maybe in Eureka.

Yes, she was a mean and cruel auntie,
Turning buildings into shanties,
Burning up houses and property,
Demanding justice, committing robbery.
Aunt Ifa was an armed vigilante.

An aunt to avoid at Thanksgiving,
She's always angry, not forgiving.
Maligns you when you've done no wrong,
She always hums an anarchy song.
An aunt eater from the beginning.

Aunt Ifa knows how to play Uncle Sam,
And Uncle Sam didn't stop her scam.
With her it's "catch and release,"
It's the "in thing" to hate the police
Her "righteous" stand is a sham.

You used to find her at the land of Chop,
Not with a squeegee and not with a mop.
But she would have spray paint cans
And stimulus checks in her hands,
Yelling profanities at all the cops.

In downtown Portland, if you go for a jog,
You will see Aunt Ifa sitting on a log,
Sitting there burning our flag.
Hanging out, smoking a drag,
Her brain cells are in a fog.

Aunt Ifa's aunt hill brings unrest.
She's based in the Pacific Northwest.
Plays the divider, not the healer.
Just ask Portland mayor, Ted Wheeler.
Starting riots in her protests.

On the news see these fire aunts.
You can hear their unruly chants.
Their mission is violence;
Media helps with silence.
Decency and order they supplant.

Auntie will bring over cocktails,
Destroy store fronts and retail,
Spreading hate and terror.
Consumed in ideological error.
Opposing views she will derail.

So Aunt Ifa still runs wild,
Never disciplined as a child.
Hoodies and dressed in black,
The innocent she will attack.
Liberty she has reviled.

I don't think Aunt Ifa is employed.
As I see more cities destroyed,
Can't others see the light?
Or is it only those on the right?
But most of us are beyond annoyed.

Prayer in a Beer Cooler

A testimony that came out of the Joplin tornado on May 22, 2011. Twenty-four people huddled in a beer cooler in a convenient store. Everything in the area was leveled to the ground except the beer cooler. In the cooler, a few people offered up some desperate prayers, and they were heard.

Years ago in Joplin, Missouri,
On a calm May day,
A tornado paved its way—
An F-5 in all its fury.

People took shelter in a beer cooler.
A few people, to Jesus, prayed
As the walls around them swayed.
The destruction could not be crueler.

Endured the F-5 roaring sound,
But the cooler was left standing,
Everything else leveled to the ground.

When they emerged and looked around,
I'm sure they gained understanding—
Answers to prayer today still abound.

Canceled in Canada

About Pastor Artur Palowski, who was put in solitary confinement in Canada for preaching to the members of the trucker blockade.

Solitary confinement
Twenty-three hours a day.
Mistreated in prison
For words he did say.

Welcome to Canada,
Land of no constitution.
Welcome to Canada,
Religious persecution.

Here come the bandits,
No law and order.
The free speech police
Right across our border.

In corrupt Canada,
There sits an iron curtain
With wicked leaders.
You can be certain.

At Canada's dictator,
I am perplexed.
My question for us now:
Will America be next?

Pancake Economy

I went out to breakfast
And my order they did take.
"I will take eggs and bacon
And add one pancake."

So the food came out.
It looked good, you see.
I ate my bacon first
Because bacon's good for me.

Then I ate my eggs;
Not long did it take.
But I just kept staring
At that one pancake.

Suddenly, it hit me,
And I started to laugh.
This pancake before me
Is our economy graph.

My wife looked at me and said,
"What are you talking about?"
I said, "This is a pancake graph.
You gotta check this out."

I grabbed my toast;
I stacked them on the wall.
"This was our economy before,
And the pancake shows our fall.

"Stimulus checks are nice
Like the pancake tastes great.
But now there's inflation,
And we've taken the bait."

Customers started staring,
So I got up on a chair.
"Everyone, please listen.
I have something to share.

"Look at my stacked toast.
That's where we were at.
Now look at my pancake.
Now we have gone flat.

"Please hold up your pancake.
I want to show this is awful.
If you don't have a pancake,
Just raise up your waffle."

All over the restaurant,
I thought it was great.
People held up pancakes,
Waffles, and even crepes.

We had a moment of silence
As people nodded their heads.
This pancake economy
Many of us fear and dread.

I sat down in my chair.
A solid point I did make.
We have moved from stacked toast
To an economic pancake.

Scam Artist

Look at the artist.
Hidden meanings he weaves
As he paints secret thieves.
Behind the trees of cedar
Crouch the evil leaders.

Look what he depicts:
Political figures concealed
Behind the media's shield.
In this painting, can you find
The blind leading the blind?

Look at the canvas
As he paints, with strokes,
The common folks.
The unknown and small,
He displays them all.

Gaze upon the wall.
The common folks you see.
Folks like you and like me.
On the canvas, they are forsaken,
In the landscape, they are taken.

See the whole picture:
The common folks, the prey.
Leaders look the other way.
They took and they took
When no one seemed to look.

So the painter paints.
Each day, more change.
Each hour, more strange.
In each brush, upheaval.
In each stroke is evil.

Look closer at the art.
Who is it that paints?
Can you feel the constraint?
Brushing away freedom
Displayed as a museum.

Do you know the meaning?
Look again at the painting.
Our purpose they are tainting.
Wolves disguised as lambs,
Masterpiece of a scam.

Gender-Neutral Potato Head

Mr. Potato Head is going gender neutral. Hasbro is dropping the Mr. from the logo and overall brand to promote gender equality and inclusion.

Mr. Potato Head is now saying goodbye.
We now have a potato head that's half girl, half guy.
In this Cancel Culture, we are being tutored,
And now Mr. Potato Head is being neutered.

I remember as a kid mixing up the potato parts.
But now this confusion is off the charts.
What if a Russet wants to change to a red potato?
What if a red potato wants to change to a tomato?

I grabbed two potatoes, and I held them in the air.
I seriously can't tell the gender of these pair.
Oh, wait! This potato is a male. I figured it out.
Oh no! Hold on. That is just a potato sprout.

Quickly, I grabbed a peeler and started peeling.
I started scanning but got an awkward feeling.
So I covered my potato in a little towel,
And I sat there and stared at it with a scowl.

I realized I can't tell the gender of a potato,
And I can't tell the gender of a cherry tomato.
And now Mr. Potato Head is a neutral gender.
I'm trying to be sensitive and not be an offender.

Hey, maybe the Hasbro name they should rename.
There is *bro* in Hasbro, in that manly name.
I don't care if their name is HasBrenda,
But this is just another man-pleasing agenda.

In Idaho, if Mr. Potato Head was born a mister,
I say we don't change it and make him a sister.
Now I have no idea if it's a mister or a sister.
All I know is Hasbro is playing gender twister.

I should introduce a competitor named Mr. Gourd.
It would come with a guitar so he can play some chords.
Listen, Mr. Gourd would be 100 percent man,
But he would be wild, you understand.

I went out to eat at Five Guys: burgers and fries.
It really bugged me that Hasbro was not wise.
Then I thought, *Should they rename Five Guys?*
As I scarfed down my gender-neutral fries.

Maybe they should rename it Five Gals
Or maybe go neutral with just Five Pals.
Or maybe they will change it to Five Trans.
I really don't know what's in their plans.

However, if they do change the name of Five Guys,
I will have to get out my set of angry eyes.
We weren't easily offended not that long ago.
We wouldn't have complained about Mr. Potato.

I'm definitely not a potato educator.
I am really only a lowly common tater.
I'm trying to share with you some tater thoughts.
I do think it's wrong what's being taught.

Mr. Potato Head heads to gender purgatory.
Next to get cancelled may be Toy Story.
This neutered potato idea needs to be trashed.
If not, those potato heads need to be mashed.

Did You Castro Vote?

Written on November 4, 2020.

Did you Castro vote?
Did you board the leftist boat?
In voting, where did Hugo?
Hugo would be so proud, you know.

Lenin give you my two cents:
Election choices come at an expense.
Lenin tell you what I think.
Lenin watch us while we sink.

Let me Putin to you in case you missed.
How is our nation Putin up with this?
Are you ill like Kim Jong-il?
Or do you have a brain still?

Do you the praises of socialism sing?
Do you want a leader like Ho Chi Minh?
With this election, did we fail?
Did we follow the steps of Mikhail?

Can you see what I Minh?
Marx on our future will be seen.
What was then has become the now,
Likeness of the leader Mao.

As the vote counting has been Stalin,
To socialism have we fallen?
Kim Jong-il or Kim Jong-un,
Will we see communism soon?

Kim Jong-un or Kim Jong-il,
Will we have a nation still?
I hope you did not Castro vote.
But will we sink, or will we float?

Trapped in Fallujah

In 2004, a group of Marines were trapped in Fallujah, Iraq, by a sandstorm called the "Churning." For three days, they were pelted by hot sand and rocks. They could hardly breathe and thought they were going to die. They desperately cried out to Jesus. After three days, they looked out and saw that the sandstorm was actually a blessing from God. The sandstorm had misplaced a deadly minefield that they would have walked right into.

Back in the year 2004,
West of Baghdad forty miles,
Marines on this desert floor
Withstood tests and trials.

In the battle of Fallujah,
From a Sergeant named Tim,
Came forth a Hallelujah
When conditions looked grim.

In the distance, an ominous sky
Threatened to engulf the men.
They could not outrun if they tried.
In quite a predicament then.

The sandstorm named the "Churning."
Soldiers trapped against the wall.
Their heads pressed and felt the burning.
"God stop this storm!" they did call.

Three days of sand and wind,
Motionless on the ground.
Three days they were pinned,
Horrific roaring sound.

Furious sandstorm persisted,
Survival looking bleak.
Storm of particulates resisted.
Stones scalded their cheeks.

Fighting for each breath,
Warring against their fears.
Now facing apparent death,
Storm of every hundred years.

Prepared to be buried alive
In the suffocating storm.
To breathe, they did strive
When blinding sand did swarm.

Three days of the "Churning."
Now it was gradually subsiding.
Three days of intense burning.
Now the men came out of hiding.

Finally able to get up and stand,
Assistance the storm did yield.
Winds misplaced so much sand,
Uncovered a deadly minefield.

Sergeant Tim now gasped
As he saw this explosive trap.
He realized and grasped
That God saw them on the map.

Underneath the desert sky,
Where those marines stood,
God had heard their desperate cry
And worked the bad for good.

Trials in your life can work for good.
He redeems what's wrecked.
Your struggles He has understood.
He is the master architect.

In life, we will go through storms,
Sometimes for days and days.
We may lose sight of His form,
But perfect are His ways.

Storms must be endured,
Even if they seem longer.
By faith, rest assured.
Storms make you stronger.

In hardships, if you feel unseen
And can't seem to raise a Hallelujah,
Remember God and those Marines
When they were trapped in Fallujah.

No "Free" Rides

In 1997 in Harare, Zimbabwe, twenty mental patients escaped from a bus. The driver offered "free rides" to replace them with sane citizens. He delivered the sane citizens to a mental hospital. It took the medical personnel three days to uncover the foul play. The real mental patients remained at large.

Some people learned the hard way
In the country of Zimbabwe.
A taxi driver offered rides for free.
The destination was hidden you see.

They enjoyed their free taxi ride,
Amazed at how easy it was supplied.
Where they were going, the driver did not explain.
Free rides to the hospital of the insane.

Their free ride led them right to a trap—
A place of confinement not on their map.
Wanting no cost and wanting no pain
Caused these people to not use their brain.

Here, today, "free" seems to be the goal.
Content with crumbs but giving up control.
So history repeats; it's nothing new
When something sounds too good to be true.

Thank God for the Fleas!

The story about Betsie and Corrie Ten Boom
as taken from The Hiding Place.

Two sisters from Holland
In their divine calling
Knew God in the present
When life was not pleasant

Fear they did not choose
When they harbored the Jews
Believed God and His Book
Though imprisoned in Ravensbruck

A cruel concentration camp
Barracks full of reeking straw
Nausea swept over them
Hundreds of women they saw

A house of suffering
Not a place of ease
Jammed in the barracks
Full of biting fleas

To answered prayer
Betsie had the keys
She bowed her head
And thanked God for the fleas

She knew God's Spirit
She drank from the fountain
She thanked Him in the valley
And she praised Him on the mountains

And because of the fleas
Guards stayed far away
They had freedom to worship
And freedom to pray

Many prisoners found God
It was not just by chance
Because Betsie thanked God
In all her circumstance

And so when life brings thorns
And gives you tests you never chose
In the middle of those thorns
Will lay a beautiful rose

The Masker Plan

One mask, two mask, three mask, four.
Will Dr. Fauci require any more?
How many masks can make a masker feel mad?
And how many masks, on my face, can I add?

Fauci says one, but now he says two.
I don't think Fauci even has a clue.
Now the land will be double masking.
Is anyone in the land double asking?

With all these masks, I can't tell who does meth,
But I am kind of glad people can't smell my breath.
He says two masks on my face will make me wiser.
How about two masks with a visor?

Here a mask; there a mask.
Everywhere a second mask, mask.
Once, twice, three masks a lady.
And all with a mask on, except Tom Brady.

One mask, two mask, three mask, four.
Now I have a mask in every drawer.
Early to bed and two masks on when you rise
Makes a man healthy, wealthy, and wise?

Now look at me. I'm better than you.
I have three masks, and you only have two.
I know that sounds holier than thou.
See the sweat pouring from my brow.

Here as I hear flip-flop Fauci,
I'm feeling more than a little grouchy.
OK, let's get some goggles like Dr. Birx said,
And then put on two masks like I read.

And let's wear these with no one in our car,
And let's wear a chem suit near and far.
The madness and stupidity do not end.
His reasoning I cannot comprehend.

You may think I'm an antimasker,
But I'm really just a question asker
Asking a question that seems legit.
At two masks will he finally quit?

All Things Work for Good

Romans 8:28: "And we know all things work together for good to those who love God, to those who are the called according to His purpose"

Life may not go as it should
God's ways can be confusing
But yet all things work for good

There are questions and there are doubts
His plans don't always make sense
But still God works things out

Through struggles and through trials
We can't always see His hand
But He walks beside us all the miles

I refuse to question Jesus above
Though He hides His plan at times
I hold on fast to His unfailing love

The enemy will come to attack
He attacks like a roaring lion
But God's plan remains on track

His dealings are not understood
When life around us shakes
But still all things work for good

Indian Burn

Regarding the Cleveland Indians changing their name to the Guardians.

In the middle of an Indian summer,
More words offend, and it gets dumber.
One hundred years of the "Indian" name,
And now all of sudden it brings shame.

Cleveland's new name, the Guardians.
I'm guessing the decision was bipartisan.
Yes, the Guardians of the MLB.
Guardians who will probably take a knee.

I guess the name brought so much grief.
I'm curious now. What about the Chiefs?
Really, what names should we save?
No one is offended by the Atlanta Braves.

To other names, we don't say goodbye.
Look at the Illinois Fighting Illini.
And what if Illinois plays Florida State?
That Indian tribe name war would bring some hate.

What about a Cowboys' name battle?
I think their name offends some cattle.
Look, I'm not trying to expose or tattle.
But will they change the name of Seattle?

Tell me, why haven't people gotten cranky
And banned those New York Yankees?
What if the name *Angels* causes people to flip out?
Because believing in angels, some have doubt.

Look, I'm not trying to throw some rocks.
But what about that weird name, Red Sox?
What if red socks were worn by an Indian chief?
What if hearing that name brings his tribe grief?

What if some are offended by the Rams?
Maybe we should change it to the Lambs,
Or they could change it to the Ewes.
These names are getting harder to choose.

Coming forward are another forty whiners,
Soon to be offended by the 49ers.
It seems our society does not learn.
We are suffering from an Indian burn.

So people listen to every demander.
We now live in the republic of pander.

Opportunity Knox

The story of Henry Knox in November 1775.

*Something is wrong and something must be done or we shall
be involved in all the horror of failure, and civil war without
a prospect of its termination.*

—*Henry Knox*

Henry Knox owned a bookstore
But he had a higher calling
Cannons he would be hauling
He would soon join the war

Over 300 miles
In only fifty-six days
There could be no delays
They pushed through the trials

He arrived at Lake Champlain
Temperature below freezing
But yet still preceding
A mission that seemed insane

Crossing the Hudson River
Knox nearly froze
In three feet of snow
Pressing on though he shiver

Not one cannon was lost
Secured all fifty-nine
These men who had a spine
For freedom counted the cost

Pressing forward with their plow
In Boston they arrived
All the men survived
Found respect from General Howe

He thought out of the box
Overcame the conditions
Amazing expedition
From opportunity Knox

Through the Fire without Burning

The story of one Iraqi Christian who stood in the face of persecution. Isis stoned him and doused him with 20 gallons of gasoline and attempting to burn him. The fire burned but he was not consumed. They tried this three times and finally released him unharmed.

Years ago in Iraq,
One Christian took a stand,
But Jesus had his back—
A miracle in the land

In this place of desert sand,
His unwavering faith was seen.
Isis took him by the hand
And doused him with gasoline.

A fire lit and all were seeing.
But as they watched, they learned—
The fire consumed his being,
But yet he was not burned.

He was saved through the fire.
Jesus's hand took him higher.

Seattle No Longer Chief

Seattle has become a mess
On the streets with the homeless.
In downtown, on each street,
Vile and shameless.

Trash and broken glass;
Tents staked in the grass;
Rocks, sticks, and bricks
Thrown from an overpass.

Villages that make you cringe
As you walk by each syringe.
Where Seattle goes from here,
That decision will hinge.

Under the guise of compassion,
A city council of inaction,
But common sense and truth
They seem to get no traction.

Costing the city a fortune,
Do they want to be like Portland?
Safety, security, and cleanliness,
It doesn't seem to be important

If you go to the gum wall to see gum,
You can see what Seattle has become,
Yet the city sits on their hands.
To reality, they have become numb.

Seattle, a haven for illegals,
No longer protecting the people.
Felons in homeless camps
Right below the Space Needle.

A once beautiful city
Now doesn't look so pretty.
Destroying itself from within,
What a shame! What a pity!

The Angel of Warsaw

Irena Sendler rescued 2,500 Jewish children from the Warsaw ghetto. In 2007, she was nominated for the Noble Peace Prize but lost to Al Gore.

Irena Sandler obeyed a higher law
The road to freedom she paved
2,500 Jewish children she saved
The amazing angel of Warsaw

Dreadful ghetto conditions she saw
Entered to smuggle children out often
Hid them in potato sacks and coffins
Brought hope to the ghetto of Warsaw

Captured by the Nazi's in 1943
Broke the bones in her legs and feet
Sentenced execution came near
Someone paid to set her free

Death she would defeat
Her bravery conquered fear

Life Is Only but a Mist

Life is only but a mist.
In each breath, the end draws near.
We can't be content to just exist.

Though struggles in this life persist
And though darkness may appear,
Life is only but a mist.

Though life's journey may turn and twist,
Trials and tests may not disappear.
We can't be content to just exist.

Having good intentions and bucket lists
Yet we can hesitate to act out of fear.
But life is only but a mist.

In following others, we must resist.
It does not matter if they jeer or cheer.
We can't be content to just exist.

Don't let God's plan for you be missed.
To His Spirit, solely tune your ear.
Life is only but a mist.
We can't be content to just exist.

When One Took on All

*The story of Private First Class Jack Hanson during
the Korean War on June 7, 1951.*

In the Korean War
In the early morning hours
A hero we can't ignore
A soldier who did not cower

When others fell back
He kept his position
He continued the attack
Held fast to the mission

One against them all
A fierce battle did rage
But he answered the call
And continued to engage

His ammo became depleted
Yet he continued to fight
He would not be defeated
He gave all of his might

No more ammo and no gun
Yet he still did remain
A whole army against one
A sacrifice not in vain

He wasn't forced to respond
Though danger was near
To the call he went beyond
This hero volunteered

The Man from Crete

There once was a man from Crete.
Name was Peter, but went by Pete.

He tried hard to be discreet
When he went to get a bite to eat.

But as he walked down the street,
Some street rioters he did meet.

They did not seem so sweet.
He tried to avoid this meet and greet.

He walked sideways and shuffled his feet.
They stood in his way and blocked old Pete.

The mob laughed as they turned up the heat.
These rioters who were paid by the elite.

Looters who loot and aren't so neat,
A little different than peaceful Crete.

Tares of our nation among the wheat,
They pushed him down to have a seat.

There Pete got punched and beat.
For no reason, they gnashed their teeth.

No consequences for beating Pete.
No discipline from the elite.

Turning a blind eye on the street
Until Pete's beating was complete.

No justice for innocent Pete.
No sympathy for the man from Crete.

We can share and post and tweet,
But over and over, the story repeats.

We've lost protection on our streets.
The innocent voice is obsolete.

Only now, racist cries of deceit
Raining down on us like sleet.

Hide the true motives under a sheet
While Marxists yell for us to retreat.

And if they continue to get paid by the elite,
Justice will continue to take a back seat.

And forgotten will be those like Pete,
And sadly, the story will again repeat.

Injustice for All

Racist evasion,
Ignorance is bliss.
Calling all a racist,
Wisdom they miss.

We are sick and tired.
We are getting weary
Of this nonsense called
Critical race theory.

Reveal their true motives.
Let's get to the core.
What some really want
Is a tragic civil war.

Justice for some.
Some play victim.
Justice concealed,
Distorted system.

Slipping down
A slippery slope,
They want to steal
Our nation's hope.

Provoking one another,
Can't they be quiet?
New season begins
Of riot after riot.

Provoking one another,
Love does decrease.
In picking up their sword,
They are dropping off peace.

So justice eludes,
And justice does fall.
Here in America,
No justice for all.

Clinging to Psalm 46

Look around, far and near. All remains is fear.
But let it not plant deep inside.
On the news, you will lose if you hear their lies.
But there's a love up above, and He still hears our cries.

Our nation's only fix is Psalm 46.
Will you let it be your guide?
The earth will quake, and the mountains shake.
But in the deluge, God is still our refuge.

He helps at the break of dawn, when all other hope is gone.
All we have to do is be still.
As truth is assaulted, God will be exalted,
Shunning fear and staying calm, clinging to this hopeful Psalm.

The nations have raged; they want us all caged.
But there's a purpose to fulfill.
In spite of the situation and the trouble in our nation,
There is a big plus: God is still with us.

Titanic Nation

A ship deemed unsinkable
Yet carried out the unthinkable.
"God can't sink this ship"
Voiced before the fateful trip.

Today, people stressed and panicked—
America, the modern-day Titanic.
Our nation begins to take on water.
The bow begins to shake and totter.

Yet America moves along.
The band plays the song.
Nearer my God to thee.
Nearer now to the sea.

The iceberg leaves a gaping hole.
Damage now takes its toll.
Lights begin flickering
As politicians keep bickering.

We are losing our speed.
Warnings we did not heed.
No nations close by
Will help us not die.

Not being sunk by enemy fire,
Being destroyed by media liars.
Roaring engines now quitting.
America, in two, is splitting.

Nations view from a distance,
Unable to offer us assistance.
Moving slower and slower,
Sinking lower and lower.

Can God sink this ship?
Will He interrupt our trip?
Is this ship unsinkable?
Will we see the unthinkable?

Hear and answer the lifeboat call.
Our pride goes before our fall.
Can't go back, we've hit the ice.
In our arrogance, we will pay the price.

So many on this ship are blamable.
Only a few lifeboat seats available.
Hurry to a lifeboat today.
There, save yourself and pray.

This Titanic, from God, has strayed.
Time to pray like we have never prayed.
"That's our only true hope," I say,
"In the coming, challenging day."

Famous Life Sayings

*Teach a dead man to vote, and he won't vote for a day.
Vote for a dead man, and he will vote for the Democratic Party.

*Government dictatorship is not a problem to be
solved but a reality to be experienced.

*The journey of 1,000 taxes begin with one Democrat.

*Colleges are like a box of chocolates. Open
it up to see who has melted inside.

*Ask not what your country can do for you. Cross the
border, and ask what America can do for you.

*A Democrat in the hand is like two named Bush.

*In the place where the tree falls, there it will lie. And in the
place where the politician speaks, there they will lie as well.

*Speak now or forever give up your peace.

*When the going gets tough, you take a mental health day off.

*Insanity is voting for Democrats over and
over and expecting different results.

*One small gas increase for man leads to one
giant inflation leap for mankind.

*Life is 10 percent what happens to you and
90 percent how the media responds.

*The sky has no limits and neither does our national debt.

Their Blood Cries from the Ground

In honor of the thirteen soldiers who died in Kabul, Afghanistan, on August 26, 2021.

Thirteen brave soldiers
Failed leadership
Twenty long years
Now a wasted trip

Our politicians rule
Play games with lives
Like a clueless child
Juggling knives

Blunder after blunder
Error after error
Pleading with evil
Negotiating with terror

President Puppet
Who feels no pain
He will not escape
From this guilt stain

Thirteen brave heroes
Betrayed by a fool
Laid down their lives
In the city of Kabul

In that forsaken land
Rises an eerie sound
It's the sound of their blood
Crying from the ground

Cemetery Rut

Behind the white church
With the steeple
Holes have been dug
For many people

Those people don't move
They stay in the ground
They stay in their rut
They don't make a sound

They can get sun
They absorb showers
Tombs decorated
With beautiful flowers

Manicured landscaping
The green grass cut
In spite of all this
They stay in their rut

Day after day
In the same room
Year after year
In the same tomb

We can live our lives
Stagnant and strange
Digging our ruts
Fighting change

We can stick to the usual
Perform the customary
Yet we will be no different
Then a beautiful cemetery

Look at the Birds

The birds don't worry.
The birds won't tremble.
They continue to sing
When they assemble.

They don't stress.
They won't make a peep.
Over finding food,
They won't lose sleep.

They won't make a tweet
Tweeting on Twitter.
How their life is bad,
Or their lot is bitter.

They live their lives
With no fear of tomorrow.
They sing, day after day,
In spite of sorrow.

They have no storehouses,
And they have no barns.
But deep inside of them,
There is no alarm.

Yet day after day,
They have learned
The early bird
Still finds the worm.

And if God feeds them,
Know what He will do.
He will provide your needs
And take care of you.

So look at the birds
When you are outside,
And if you look to Him,
Your hand He will guide.

Cashless Society

A tribute to Johnny Cash

Present-day singers gain notoriety,
But currently we live in a Cashless society.
Today's music is mostly pop trash.
We are missing the legend Johnny Cash.

In his songs, he was a teacher.
He said more than most preachers.
Words that sometimes warned me,
The whirlwind is in the thorn tree.

To the arrogant, he voiced a sound.
He said, "God's gonna cut you down."
If he were alive today, would it be true?
Would he be banned from singing "A Boy Named Sue"?

Yes, the world is missing the "Man in Black."
Substance in his songs, he did not lack.
And to some of his quotes, I have to nod—
Like "my arms are too short to box with God."

As this world continues to spiral down,
Like Johnny said, "The man will come around."

M&M's Have Gone Woke

M&M's melt in your mouth and in your hand.
They've gone woke all across the land.
Gender identity has been nixed,
And the M&M's just got fixed.

Green candy can change to brown too,
And red candy can identify as blue.
Gender neutral and all that jive
With red 40 and yellow 5.

What if yellow 5 wants to identify as red 40?
And can one identify as tall and not be a shorty?
I always liked the chocolate with the crispy,
But now it's chocolate confused and wispy.

The M&M in my hand wants to fly solo.
He told me he identifies as a Rolo.
I said, "Huh, is this some kind of joke?"
"No, us M&M's, we've all gone woke."

To be honest, when I bought a bag from a vendor,
I opened it up and never thought of gender.
I never thought of an inclusive attack.
I just wanted some candy for a snack.

I would throw them in the air and catch them with my chops.
Everyone around would give me props.
I could catch popcorn, but I don't want to choke.
And Orville Redenbacher will probably go woke.

Sometimes I would attempt to catch red grapes.
When I caught one, I'd beat my chest like an ape.
My friends would laugh and think it's funny.
Then I would stuff my mouth and play chubby bunny.

What is going on in this crazy world?
I don't care if candy is a boy or a girl.
Before common sense goes away,
Can someone please keep wokeism at bay?

Don't even get me started with gummy bears
And what their gender is or what they wear.
Unfortunately, we are being led by a bunch of dummies.
Just leave me alone, and let me eat my gummies.

Game of Checkers

Regarding the Facebook fact-checkers.

Check, check. One, two, three.
Check, check. They disagree.
Checkers move across the board—
Pieces moving in one accord.
Checkers jumping in the fight,
Checkers choking posts of the right.

Checkers checking in the dark.
Checkers checking, leaving their mark—
Leaving their mark for leader Mark.
These fact-checkers have lit a spark.
Checker chiefs anointed by Mark,
Chewing up our posts like a shark.

Chugga, chugga, chugga, choo choo.
The fact-checking train is coming for you.
Game of checkers, game of beliefs.
Post inspectors, post-stealing thieves.
Facebook and Twitter, no common sense,
Censoring and constructing a liberal fence.

Twitter tweaks and terminates our tweets.
'Twas Twitter talkers tossed liberal treats,
Trippin' and flippin' out in their blame.
Trippin' and slippin' in this checkers game,
Checkers in their biased acts.
Checkers who don't check their facts.

Listen up, Facebook fact-checkers!
You fact-checkers are freedom wreckers.
Fact-checking with a liberal twist,
Chubby Checker might say you missed.
But before you just assume you scored
King me, I moved again, across your board.

May We Never Forget

May we never forget that day in September.
Americans fallen we will always remember.
You and I recall those lost.

We know freedom comes at a cost.
Everyday heroes we did see,

Not forgetting those on Flight 93
Entering the cockpit, sacrificing all.
Valor and courage answering the call.
Even now, as our athletes kneel,
Remembering those families and how they feel.

First responders, heroes who never returned,
Offering their lives into the buildings that burned,
Running into those doomed twin towers,
Giving their life in those fateful hours.
Every fallen tear seen from Jesus in heaven.
Today we humbly remember 9/11.

The Streets of Tehran

The persecuted Christian church of Iran.

Join me and walk the streets of Tehran.
If you listen intently, you will hear a song,
And in the whispers of the wind,
You can hear the cries once again.

If you can gaze out a little higher,
Across walls topped with barbed wire,
Through the walls of windowless cells,
In the Evin prison is where they dwell.

In this prison, year after year,
Known for torture and for fear,
This underworld of destitution
Constant floggings and executions.

Across the way, in Building 209.
Prisoners' morale does decline
Under an intense cruel burden,
Sleeping under blankets of urine.

Constant threats and accusations
Under continual interrogations.
You will find a people all around.
You will find the church of the underground.

Yet their suffering turns into strength,
Willing to suffer at any length.
Under pressure beyond measure
But still Jesus is their treasure.

And as the dust blows through Tehran,
If you listen closely, you will hear a song.
And in the whispers of the wind,
You will hear their testimonies rise again.

Facts are Stubborn Things

"Facts are stubborn things,"
A wise man once said.
Lies are given wings
When the media is dead.

Balanced and fair?
Only half reported,
Biased everywhere,
Twisted, and distorted.

"Ignore those stubborn things,"
The news media said.
Puppets on the strings,
Controlled and led.

Common sense sinking
Like the Titanic.
Media does the thinking,
Creating the panic.

Fighting truth, that's what they do.
Day after day, we've seen.
Let me introduce you
To the brainwashing machine.

Lies replace truth.
Myths replace facts.
Blind, deceived youth
Going off the tracks.

Impartial and objective
Creates the illusion.
Biased perspective
Handed over to delusion.

Facts are stubborn things.
One thing that's strange:
New beliefs you can bring,
But facts never change.

Hearing what wise men wrote
Throughout our early years,
We should listen to their quotes
And not have itching ears.

"Facts are stubborn things,"
A wise man once said.
Freedom truth brings
From the lies we are fed.

Hurricane Warning

Feel the wind;
See the trees.
Don't mistake the gentle breeze.

Sea levels rise,
Ominous clouds.
Hear the urgent warning out loud.

Barometers drop,
Waves' whitecaps.
Destruction comes with our collapse.

Eerie calm,
Distant form.
Can you see the approaching storm?

Ocean's swell,
Strong riptides.
Darkness stretches miles wide.

Exposed land,
Stars and stripes
Hours before the hurricane strikes.

Prepare now;
Leave the beach.
For to us all, the storm will reach.

Stimulus for Free

The remake of "Islands in the Stream" by Dolly Parton and Kenny Rogers.

Daily, when I met you,
There were freebies unknown.
I set out to get you
So I could stay at home.

I was soft inside.
Free money I came upon.
You give something to me
That I can't explain.
I do nothing, and it's in my bank.
No job I have to start.
Living off another is the bomb.

To hard work, I'm blind.
It requires no education.
All our future, we steal
From the next generation.
They'll provide it forever, ha ha.
Video gaming with each other, ah-ha.

Stimulus for free,
That is what we need.
No hard work for me.
How can this be wrong?
Mail it now to me.
I'm in a different world,
And we rely on the government, ah-ha.
Take from one and give to another, ah-ha.

I can't live without you
If the money was gone.
Everything is something
If you got a man bun.
And I just troll all the right,
Slowly losing sight of reality.

But prices won't go up,
And I got no doubt.
Too dependent and we got no way out.
And the message is clear:
Living free is the real thing.

At no jobs, I apply.
Maybe I will work never,
Laying out in the sun.
We're in this together.
They'll provide it forever, ha ha.
Video gaming with my mother, ah-ha.

Stimulus for free,
That is what we need.
No hard work for me.
How can this be wrong?
Mail it now to me.
I'm in a different world,
And we rely on the government, ah-ha.
From one governor to another, ah-ha.

Sensitivity Training 101

"Welcome to Sensitivity Training 101.
Class, please take your seats. This should be fun.
At work, when clocked in, you must remember
Some very important things about gender.

"If there is a him, you can address him as him,
Unless the him wants to be a her or if the him is not sure.
Now if the her is a her but wants to be neutral,
Just mumble the word *her*. I hope this is useful.

"Now if the him wants to change and identify as a dog,
Then notify your supervisor for that will have to be logged.
Now if the her was a him but went back to a her and you aren't sure,
You can flip a coin, or you just go by what they were.

"If there is a man who is fifty but identifies as twenty-three,
You can meet in the middle at thirty-seven, you see.
Now if he complains and makes it an issue,
Hand that mansy pansy a box of tissues.

"Now if there is a woman who identifies as a stalk of corn
And she claims to be planted but never born,
I guess with this corny person you don't adorn.
Send them over to Nebraska in the morn.

"Now this sensitivity training will help you be awake,
Keeping you from melting all the snowflakes.
Now, class, together let's say the word *woke*."
"WOKE!"
"Great job, class. You are listening to what I spoke.

"As a baby needs their bottle,
All beliefs need be coddled.
At all costs, we must not offend.
In pandering, there is no end.

"Please sign off on this mamby pamby creed.
This next generation is a different breed."

The Days of Noah

Let's reminisce about a story of old,
About a tenacious man who was so bold.
Men scorned, ridiculed, and mocked.
They laughed at Noah while he talked,
But by faith, Noah built the ark.

He spoke to them, warning after warning.
He pleaded with them morning after morning.
Yet they mocked in the shadow of the ark,
Before the rain fell and sky grew dark,
But by faith Noah built the ark.

They shut their eyes, thought he was extreme,
Thought he was blinded by a dream.
They ignored him and sealed their fate,
And when the rain fell, it was too late.
But Noah was safe in the ark.

When the rains fell, the ark was lifted.
Outside, remained all the wicked.
And in our present world of crisis,
Will God still find some righteous
In these days of Noah?

See, you don't have to travel to Turkey
To gaze upon God's ark of mercy.
You don't have to build a large boat
To walk with God and stay afloat
In these days of Noah.

What will you and I become?
Like Noah, will we live for the One?
The earth will soon be shaken to the core.
Soon God Himself will shut the door
In these days of Noah.

Terror in Tenerife

This poem is a testimony about a man named Norman Williams, who survived history's worst airline accident. It took place at the Los Rodeos Airport in the Canary Islands on March 27, 1977. Two 747s collided with each other on the runway, and 583 people died. Only sixty-one survived, Norman among them.

There comes a testimony
Out of much sorrow and grief,
In the Canary Islands,
On the island of Tenerife.

In March 1977,
Death to many came faster.
583 died
In the worst air disaster.

In the shadow of a volcano,
The airport did reside.
A calm and peaceful day
Before the two planes collide.

Two 747s,
One pilot's tragic decision
Ended in tragedy
In a runway collision.

On the KLM jet,
All 248 died.
On the Pan Am jet,
Only sixty-one survived.

A man, Norman Williams,
Was one of the sixty-one.
Supernaturally protected
Whose time on earth was not done.

Massive explosions,
Situation looked dire.
Surrounded by flames,
But not consumed by the fire.

Passengers in front of him,
Passengers to the side,
Friends behind him,
They all burned and died.

When suddenly slammed down
By hurling debris,
He remembered the Word:
Words of Isaiah 43.

In that chapter and verse 2,
He had once learned
Through the fire you will walk,
But you will not be burned.

He cried out to Jesus
As the cabin turned black,
Spotted a hole in the ceiling
As he lay there on his back.

How could he get there?
The ceiling was too high.
Suddenly he found himself there.
Suddenly he was outside.

Raptured for a moment,
Translated in time,
God took him to the opening.
He did not have to climb.

Norman felt God's presence,
Felt something from heaven
Miraculously got him out,
Out of that 747.

Landed on the wing,
Then jumped thirty-five feet.
Shattered his ankle
When the ground he did meet.

Hurried from the wreckage,
Forced his body in motion.
Got only fifty feet away,
Then two final explosions.

We will all go through fire.
We will all go through grief.
But remember Norman Williams
In his hours at Tenerife.

He walked through the flames
And stood on God's Word.
Through all the shock and confusion,
His prayers were heard.

Even in this challenging time,
We turn over a new leaf.
But even in our fire,
God is in our Tenerife.

The Chronicles of San Francisco

Let us open up the San Fran scrolls.
To the Bay City, let's take a stroll.
Here in the land of the democrat mule,
You will see how the homeless rule
Tent cities and scattered stool.

Yes, this may not be Connecticut,
But can people have some etiquette?
In the shadow of all the steeples
Lies trash and a bunch of needles
And the homes of many illegals.

When you arrive, bring pepper spray
To the city called Baghdad by the Bay.
And as you head out to a ridge
To see the iconic Golden Gate Bridge,
Know Frisco's gone cuckoo just a smidge.

If you happen to be frisked in Frisco,
It would be in a tent city, not at a disco;
In a village with no showers
With a smell that overpowers,
Not with a scent of flowers.

Welcome to Frisco of the modern day.
Those who live there shouldn't stay.
As the homeless they try to coddle,
All around trash and broken bottles.
Not a great clean city model.

Now I roll up my San Fran scrolls,
And I haven't even told the whole.
I think San Fran missed its calling.
What is seen now is so appalling.
From the heights, this city has fallen.

America the Lighthouse

In the black of night
Stood a beacon of hope.
A lifeline, a saving rope,
Shone forth a bright light.

Now that light grows dim,
Losing its former glory.
Is this now the end of the story?
The future looks so grim.

Darkness veils the rocks.
The world now sees a faint light
As each evil man mocks.

Liberty, from our land, walks.
We must fervently pray in our fight
As God at the lighthouse door knocks.

Prayer That Changed the Wind

A testimony of the missionary Hudson Taylor.

In the year 1854,
A sailing vessel blown toward the shore.
The captain stood in disbelief
As they sailed toward the sunken reefs.

We've done everything that can be done.
Hope of survival there was none.
The wind provided no assistance.
Cannibals were seen in the distance.

Disaster the men could foresee.
Cannibals started fires with glee,
But a man named Hudson on the vessel
Said, "Let me go pray; I will go wrestle."

He grabbed three others to agree.
They called to God on bended knee,
And as they prayed on their knees,
They called to God to send a breeze.

As they prayed, there was a change:
Something peculiar, something strange.
Through prayer, God changed the wind,
Though against the wall, they were pinned.

To the sunken rocks, they did not reach.
To the dismay of those on the beach,
They did not become another man's meal.
Instead, by faith, they knew God was real.

America sails today toward the rocks.
We can argue, and we can have talks.
But there's one answer to change the breeze:
Willing vessels who stay on their knees.

Toward the reefs, we pick up speed,
But there's still time to pray and intercede.
In fervent prayer, we must chose to stand,
Or we will find ourselves on sinking sand.

Hijacked

The engines stall and wings sway.
This nation doesn't feel right today.

In our country, we begin to dive.
Losing altitude, will we arrive?

Sweat drops from my brow.
What is happening in the cockpit now?

Diving, then climbing, and diving again.
Something more than a contrary wind.

Is the first officer and pilot on hand?
Passengers around me don't understand.

Many in our nation continue to sleep.
Ignorant, we are in a dive so steep.

Do I make believe everything is fine?
Look out the window and pass the time?

The cockpit is normally secure and locked.
But now it's wide open, and I'm not shocked.

Suddenly two men enter with an evil grin.
No resistance to go walk right in.

The pilot is no longer at the controls.
Who is in charge of all the souls?

Soon an announcement in this plane jam packed:
"This is your captain speaking. We have been hijacked."

The Bear of the North

About Russia rising up to invade the Ukraine.

In the woods, false tranquility.
In the quiet, there's instability.
She lurks behind the willow trees.
She prowls silently, yet no one sees.

Spotting weakness with her eyes,
And in this hour, she will rise.
The birds up high sing a chorus,
Concealing the danger of the forest.

The bear's arrival is very near.
Her imminent rising up many fear.
While our media points their finger,
In the darkness, the bear does linger.

Yet still the bear hunts alone.
Through the years, she has grown.
She continues to stalk her prey
While our country sees decay.

It seems we are asleep in our demise.
In our distractions, she will surprise.
As our leaders find another to blame,
The bear advances, not playing games.

In the woods, concealed in the fog,
There lies the bear—the land of gog.

1939

To the tune of "1999" by Prince.

I was dreaming when I wrote this.
Forgive me if it goes astray.
But when I woke up in 2020,
Could have sworn it was judgment day.
The sky was all purple.
There were looters runnin' everywhere,
Trying to cause destruction.
You know, I don't think they cared.

Say, say two thousand, two, zero. Party over.
Oops, out of time.
So tonight, it's time to wake up like it's 1939.

I was shopping when I wrote this.
Forgive me if I shop too fast.
But I gotta buy some bacon
In case bacon doesn't last.
Riots all around us, my mind says, *prepare to fight.*
Not gonna drive to downtown Indy tonight.

Say, say two thousand, two, zero. Party over.
Oops, out of time.
So tonight, it's time to wake up like it's 1939.
Yeah, yeah. Hey.

Lemme tell you something:
If you are not going to wake up,
Don't bother knockin' at my door.
I got change in my pocket,
But I can't use it at the store.
Yeah. Hey.
Yeah, 2020s not the bomb.
Something new every day.
Time to hurry down to Costco
To stock up chili and save.
"Oh," they say.

Two thousand, two, zero. Voting's over.
Oops, out of time.
(We're runnin' out of time.)
So tonight, we need to wake up like it's 1939.
Buy Charmin like it's 1939.
Say one more time.
Two thousand, two, zero. Party over.
Oops, out of time.
So tonight, we need to wake up like it's 1939.

Alright 1939.
You say it: 1939.
Mmm, 1939.
(Ow, 1939.)

You Can't Land on the Clouds

Those clouds white and puffy
They look so soft and fluffy
And if you jump from up high
And soar fast through the sky
Soaring faster toward a town
Those clouds won't slow you down

An appearance of land
But less stable than sand
On impact you won't bounce
They cannot hold one ounce
Illusion of stability
Yet void of reality

But I hear voices out loud
Saying we can land on clouds
They will spend until they can't
Then they blame others in their rant
They turn races against each other
Shunning love for our brother

It doesn't matter how thick clouds are
They cannot hold us near or far
Politicians aim for the clouds
But yet disaster they've allowed
Refusing to obey their own rules
Professing to be wise they became fools

Landing gear retracted and the flaps set
Wheels to clouds have almost met
Fantasies embraced by some
We know this obvious outcome
Leaders attempt it and hope for the best
Where even an eagle can't make its nest

See America try to land on the clouds
Lies embraced as truth have been allowed
Flying through the white mist
In our deception we persist
But no matter the belief of the crowds
You still cannot land on the clouds

The Esau Generation

Today in our nation
Stands an Esau generation
Impatient and demanding
Instant gratification

Doing whatever feels right
Deciding with their eyes
And just like Esau of old
They choose what is not wise

For one single meal
Esau sold his birthright
Left value for pleasure
Nearsighted eyesight

What was seen in Genesis
Is seen again in the present
In our schools and colleges
In our youths and adolescents

A way that seems right
They forsake all morality
In standing against evil
They have chosen neutrality

The Esaus are everywhere
Lines vanished in the sand
Selfish and self-seeking
They fill up our land

Only living in the now
No thought to what was then
Veiled from true wisdom
Blinded again and again

They reject correction
Experiment with pleasure
No limits or boundaries
No weights or measures

Hidden are the Jacobs
We only see Esaus
Throwing off all rules
Freedom from the laws

And in this crucial hour
Stand up for what is right
Don't become an Esau
Don't sell your birthright

The Death of the Worker Bee

Something strange has happened, you see.
We've seen the death of the worker bee.
Stores close while these bees rest,
Content to stay home in their nest.

No more flying this bee does.
Neglected purpose has lost his buzz.
No more working, nor do they roam.
They've been paid to stay at home.

Scared of predators, at home they linger.
They seem to forget they have a stinger.
With every excuse, they are falling,
Embracing laziness—a missed calling.

Yet some worker bees do go to work
While these resting bees stay home with a smirk.
These workers have to work harder and faster
While their nest becomes an economic disaster.

Handout after handout with free money.
No toil required for that free honey.
Those in charge have created, you see,
The tragic death of the worker bee.

Mad in Madison

On February 20, 2022, Juwan Howard (coach of the Michigan Wolverines) hit one of the Wisconsin coaches after they lost their game.

I saw, yesterday in Madison,
A coach who was mad a ton.
He should have been mad at none.
But he hit a coach, and that was dumb.

Now what's his excuse in Madison?
Lost his temper after a game of basketball,
He shouldn't have blown a gasket at all.
I'm wondering: Did the mascot fall?

All I know is he has no class at all.
Time for him to leave coaching basketball.
Now with this coach over at Michigan,
He probably shouldn't see a swish again.

All because he went and hit a chin.
I'm thinking they should dismiss within.
I'm waiting for the response out of Michigan.
It's too bad for this year's Wolverines.

There wasn't a very good role model seen.
To a lot of us, it is getting old. I mean,
Now they'll probably have a losing team.
What a poor sport from the Wolverines.

Pastor Pansy

Presenting Pastor Pansy to preach.
Pitiful preaching week after week.
Pansy picked a pack of polished pastors
Preaching to please people, bringing disaster.

Playing games, man pleasing.
Frozen chosen; they are freezing.
More poor, pretty preaching.
More problematic teaching.

Pansies softening the message they preach.
Pillow prophets who give their speech.
Avoiding politics is Pastor Pansy,
Preaching with clarity like a chimpanzee.

Powerless proclamations polluted.
Puppet's pandering words diluted.
More than preachers, we need prophets.
No more pastors who pick the pockets.

Pansies that won't preach against sin.
Mamby Pamby congregation within.
Pastor Pansy won't pay the price.
Pastor Pansy is way too nice.

Bye, Bye to the Media Lies

The remake of the song "American Pie" by Don McLean, this was written in the summer of 2020, during the rioting of our major cities.

A long, long time ago,
I can still remember how the fake news was not so vile.
Now if they had their chance, America would become like France,
And maybe they'd be happy for a while.

But February made me shiver
Before Wuhan did deliver
COVID-19 at our doors,
Closing down all the stores.

I could not tell who had lied.
Media covered up and denied.
Someone high up tried to hide
The day our freedom died.

So bye, bye to the media lies.
In my Chevy, I got heavy eating burgers and fries.
And those fake news anchors, I believe, were high,
Singin' let's not let America die.
America's too young to die.

Have you read the book of love, and do you have faith in God above?
The Bible does tell us so.
This year at the election polls, can a president save your mortal soul?
Mail in votes delivered really slow.

In North Korea, there's some guy named Kim
Who wants our future to look grim.
Makes me want to kick off my shoes,
Watch Top Gun with Tom Cruise.

Those Democrats have run amok
With Pelosi and some guy named Chuck.
They think we are out of luck
The day our freedom died.

I started singin' bye, bye to the media lies.
In my Chevy, I got heavy eating burgers and fries.
And them good ol' boys refused to comply,
Singin' we can't let America die.
America's too young to die.

For the last ten years, we've been on our phones
While the politicians cast their stones,
But that's not how it used to be.
Before Michael Jackson sang Billie Jean,
Before we were addicted to our screens,
To honor the flag, we were free.

Oh and while our cities were burning down,
The liberal mayors played the clown.
Common sense was spurned.
Are we even concerned?

And while our youth read a book on Marx,
Antifa camped out in the park.
Molotov cocktails lit a spark
The day our freedom died.

We were singin'
Bye, bye the media lies.
In my Chevy, paid the tax levy that I despised.
Those good ole boys spoke out against our demise,
Singin' we can't let America die.
America is too young to die.

Helter-skelter in a summer swelter.
Is it time to go to the fallout shelter?
American dream is fading fast.
Business owners left with broken glass.
Protesters who showed no class.
No reporting on the CNN newscast.

Now Chicago's streets were doom and gloom,
And Portland's streets had a smoky plume.
Seattle gave Chop a chance.
Minneapolis had its last dance.

'Cause the athletes that came and kneeled,
But a few of them refused to yield.
Ratings soon to be revealed
The year the anthem died.

We started singin' bye, bye to the media lies.
In my Chevy, my heart was heavy listening to those guys.
Politicians were wolves in disguise,
Singin' we can't let America die.
America is too young to die.

College students were all in one place.
A generation lost in space.
Professors brainwashing again.
Oh, Jack be nimble; Jack think quick.
And Jack turn off that Netflix
'Cause Netflix is the devil's friend.

Toward conservatives were fits of rage.
Night protesters were paid a wage.
Now look, our cities fell,
Revealed by Soro's spell.

And as the flames climbed high into the night,
Reparations didn't seem quite right.
I saw Satan laughing with delight
The day our freedom died.

I started singin' it: Bye, bye to the media lies.
Paid the levy in my Chevy but the levy was high.
Them good ol' boys waved the flag up high,
Singin' we can't let America die.
America is too young to die.

I met a girl who sang the blues,
And I asked her for some happy news.
But she just smiled and turned away.
Our voice, now, must become a roar.
Marxism knocking at our door,
But many preachers just look the other way.

In the streets where the prophets dreamed,
The silent majority lit up and beamed.
The courageous word was spoken
Though some church bells were broken.

And the God I admire most,
The Father, Son, and Holy Ghost,
We need Him from coast to coast
The day our freedom died.

And we were singin' bye, bye to the antifa rise.
In my Chevy, eyes were heavy from the smoke in my eyes.
Them good ol' boys prayed to Jesus on high,
Singin' we can't let America die.
America is too young to die.

Bye, bye to the media lies.
In my Chevy, my heart was heavy because the end was nigh.
Them good ol' boys prayed to Jesus on high,
Singin we can't let America die.
We can't let America die.

My Sofa's Away from Me

A parody of "So Far Away from Me" by Dire Straits in regard to the labor shortage, this must be sung from the back of your throat while hardly moving your lips.

Here I am at this same old job,
And my sofa's away from me.
And where is an employee when the sun comes up?
And my sofa's away from me.

My sofa's away from me.
It's so far away, I just can't see.
My sofa's away from me.
My sofa's away from me, all right!

I'm tired of being at work and bein' all alone.
My sofa's away from me.
I'm tired of interviewing on the telephone
'Cause my sofa's away from me.

My sofa's so far away from me,
And I get so tired of employees with no brain
When my sofa's away from me.
See, they've been on their couch, and I've been in the rain.
Yeah, my sofa's away from me.

My sofa's away from me.
They're so far, I just can't see.
My sofa's away from me/
It's so far away from me; take the indeed ad down.

Where Art Thou, Good Employee?

Where art thou, good employee?
Thou art hidden from me.
Where art thou, good employee?
Wither thou too lazy?

To see or not to see?
That is the question.
To get back to work.
Yeah, that is my suggestion.

Thy love hard work.
Thy love work not.
Thou hard earned paycheck
Thou hast not sought.

Thy love thy unemployment.
All that glitters is not gold.
Betrayed by thy handouts,
Which hath not been told.

Wherewithal and where are all?
Are those who, for jobs, doeth fight?
But now, in the array of the internet world,
All the youth art glued to Fortnight.

Employee, employee? Where art thou, employee?
How hast thou paid thy rent?
Verily, thy money will disappear.
Soon is the winter of your discontent.

Employee, employee, let down thy hair.
Wilt thou be a loyal tech?
We looketh past thy drug convictions
And thy tattoos upon thy neck.

Wither ye, hither ye, slither ye.
Working is such sweet sorrow.
Hast not another ither thee?
Wilt thou skippeth thy interview tomorrow?

Employee, employee, get out of thy chair.
Thou hast not brought good cheer.
Time ticketh away in thy life.
Thou sitteth too long on thy rear.

He Will Give His Angels Charge

In 1967, an Israeli soldier was protected by angels from the Syrians during the Six-Day War. Syrian soldiers reported to UN officials that they had seen thousands of angels surrounding this injured soldier and had, therefore, fled.

A miracle in the Six-Day War.
Fighting in the Golan Heights,
The Syrians saw some sights
They had never seen before.

Ambushed and run over by a tank,
A soldier lay paralyzed,
Surrounded and terrified,
But he had God to thank.

Suddenly he saw a light.
The Syrians turned and ran.
Angels surrounded this man—
Thousands dressed in white.

Can we learn from this soldier?
When God can seem withdrawn,
Yet He shows up when hope is gone.
He is our future holder.

Our faith we must enlarge.
Your calling is not done.
Hold on to Psalm 91.
He will give His angels charge.

Vision in the Night

Fanny Crosby wrote 9,000 hymns in spite of her blindness.
She said, "It is not enough to have a song on your lips.
You must also have a song in your heart."

Fanny Crosby you may not know
Her story should be told
9,000 hymns written to show
Though blind from six weeks old

Her love for God was bold
She wrote seven hymns a day
To the world she was not sold
The victim she would not play

In her adversity she made a way
In self-pity she could have wallowed
She spoke to presidents in her day

Not complaining to God she followed
She prevailed in life without her sight
Fanny had vision in the dark of night

Asleep in Sodom

The city of Sodom;
The city of Gomorrah.
Planting and building you see,
But when the fire fell,
They perished suddenly.

They had fullness of food,
Abundance of idleness
Seen in Ezekiel 16.
The sin of their pride
Consumed by their routine.

Living for themselves,
Consumed by pleasure.
Evil was called good,
Unaware of coming doom,
Not living like they should.

They ate and they drank.
They bought and they sold.
Working but yet asleep,
Sin was their quicksand.
They were stuck in it deep.

Are we awake today?
And are we listening?
America seems so odd.
We are busy yet asleep.
We have turned our backs on God.

Modern day Sodom;
Present day Gomorrah.
"Forgive us, Lord," we pray.
"Make us hear the alarm.
Turn us back today."

Will we hit rock bottom
Or the depths of despair
Before there is a cry?
Will we need fire to respond?
America's too young to die.

Modern day Sodom
America has recreated.
May we turn before it's too late?
We need a spiritual awakening
To spread from state to state.

The mockers will mock.
The wicked will shout,
But Jesus still reigns.
May we have ears to hear
In a time of birthing pains.

The Social Media Sound of Silence

The Remake of "The Sound of Silence" by Simon and Garfunkel.

Hello Facebook, my old friend.
I've come to post with you again.
Conservative posts you are sweeping,
Removed our posts when we were sleeping.
And the poem that was planted in my brain,
Still remains
Within the sound of silence.

And in the naked light, I saw
10,000 posts. Maybe more.
People posting but not speaking.
Facebook hearing but not listening.
People writing posts that Facebook never shares,
And no one dared
Disturb the sound of silence.

Zuckerberg said, "I you do not know."
Silence, like a cancer, grows.
Hear my words that I might teach you,
Because soon my words will not reach you.
But my words, like silent raindrops, fall,
Echoed in the Facebook walls of silence.

And the people bowed and prayed
While, every post, Facebook weighed.
And the sign flashed out its warning:
What Mark Zuckerberg was forming.
Soon the words of the prophets will have to be written on the subway walls
Or in tenement halls
And whispered in the sounds of silence.

Old-Time Freedom

The Remake of "Old Time Rock and Roll" by Bob Seger.

Take those old history books off the shelf.
I'll sit and read them by myself.
These leaders don't have the same soul.
They love their power and control.

Don't try to take me to San Francisco.
I can't count homeless people no more.
They seem to be shutting down every store.
I like that old-time freedom, you know.

Still like that old-time freedom, you know.
That kind of vision just soothes my soul.
I reminisce about the days of old
With that old-time freedom, you know.

Won't listen to their socialist lingo.
I'd rather hear from some old veteran I know.
There's only one place that I want to go:
To hang out with those who love freedom, you know.

Call me a relic; call me what you will.
Say I'm old fashioned and I'm over the hill.
These leaders don't have the same soul.
I love that old-time freedom, you know.

Fauci and Lefty

To the tune of "Pancho and Lefty" by Willie Nelson; Lefty is Bill Gates.

Livin' on Corona, my friend,
Wasn't gonna keep us free, you mean.
And now wearing my mask, I'm tired,
And my breath is hard as kerosene.

Were you the left's decoy?
Their favorite one, it seems.
Now we all want to say goodbye
To all your COVID team.

Fauci was a two-mask boy.
His voice was hoarse and yet so real.
He wore a mask as he panted
For all the honest world to feel.

Fauci left his mask, you know,
On the deserts, down in Mexico.
We all have heard his lyin' words.
Oh, but that's the way it goes.

All the credibles, they say
With our lives, he likes to play.
They only let him slip away
Out of kindness, I suppose.

Lefty likes to sing the blues
All day long about the flu.
The vaccine Fauci talked about,
Spoken out from Lefty's mouth.

Can't they let poor Fauci go?
Send him out to Ohio.
Where he got the COVID stats to show,
There ain't nobody knows.

All the credibles, they say
He just flip-flops every day.
They only let him slip away
Out of kindness, I suppose.

This poet tells how Fauci's stats don't gel,
And Lefty's livin' in grand hotels.
Concerts are quiet, and masks are old.
And so the story ends, we're told.

Facui needs your prayers, it's true.
Save a few for Lefty too.
We always knew they had no clue,
And now they're growin' old.

All the credibles, they say
With our lives, he likes to play.
They let him continue to be wrong
Out of kindness, I suppose.

The Hero of Lexington

The story of Samuel Whittemore, a hero of the Revolutionary War.

The year was 1775.
A farmer with the heart of a lion
Somehow escaped alive.
To fear, he did not buy in.

At age seventy-eight, he hid behind a wall.
Bold, brave, and not skittish,
Grabbed his musket and stood tall.
Took out three of the British.

One man versus them all,
He took no thought of his age.
Refused to hide behind the wall,
A highlight on freedom's page.

Shot in the face and bayoneted,
It looked like he wouldn't survive.
He gave his all and had no regrets.
Somehow he made it out alive.

They said his wounds they could not fix,
But this bold lion had some fight.
He lived eighteen more years, to age ninety-six.
He was a light that burned so bright.

A brave soldier of a different generation,
Whittmore, at seventy-eight, gave all for our nation.

Snowflakes in October

Why are there snowflakes in October?
It doesn't even feel cold all over.
I saw some melting at a Target store
When a mask didn't cover a nose anymore.

Have you seen them melt again and again?
I saw one melt because a bathroom door said *men*.
I'm not seeing a snowman or an ice igloo.
See they melt so fast; it's what they do.

They say no two snowflakes look alike,
But to argue that, I really just might.
The big flakes fall, just look around,
But they melt the moment they hit the ground.

They don't unify to make a snow angel,
But toward authority, they are disdainful.
I'm not out of my mind; I'm truly sober.
But I did see snowflakes in October.

Maskless in Miami

A priest, a genie, and AOC walk into a bar,
Not in New York but somewhere kind of far.
The priest had three wishes from the genie,
While AOC sat down and drank her martini.

The priest asked loudly for all to hear.
He wanted one bourbon, one scotch, and one beer.
AOC looked at the genie but had nothing to ask.
The genie said, "Are you sure you don't need a mask?"

She said, "No, tonight I'm feeling kind of pretty.
Plus Omicron only stays in New York City."
The genie tilted his head and stared at her booze.
He said, "Aren't you the one who complained about Ted Cruz?"

"Yeah, remember when he went to Cancun?
You were the one growling like a raccoon."
She said, "No, that was a different kind of vacation."
The genie said, "Uh, maybe you need some reeducation.

"I may not be the fairest of them all,
But I can spot a hypocrite sitting tall.
See, you speak one thing and do another,
And then the truth you try to smother.

"I assume you'll have a childlike fit,
But you are truly the definition of a hypocrite."
He said, "Look, I have a mirror I can supply,
It will help you see the log in your own eye."

She said, "No, I'm fine. I can see.
I will just go and blame the GOP."
She was getting mad; she was getting annoyed.
She said, "You can't tell me where to avoid."

The genie noticed the bar was a little cramped.
He said, "I'm sorry. I have to go find my lamp."
He said, "Listen, AOC, no hard feelings in the least.
Enjoy your vacation in the beautiful Southeast.

"Look, as a gift, here is a DeSantis mug."
And he then disappeared on his magic rug.

Blast in Beirut

On August 4, 2020, the Beirut explosion occurred at the Port of Beirut. Pastor Saeed Deeb ran the Life Center Church a mile away from the epicenter, where they were cooking food for refugees. A prompt from the Holy Spirit caused him to shut everything down and send everyone home.

In Beirut, an explosion
But one man divinely chosen.
Ammonium nitrate was stored,
But he was protected by the Lord.

At a mission, Pastor Deeb entered
Where he ran the Life Center,
But on this day August 4,
He felt an uneasiness come forth.

An uneasiness in his spirit,
From the Spirit, he did hear it.
"Shut it down"—the words he heard.
Everyone thought it was absurd.

They fed the hungry and were cooking food,
But now Pastor Deeb seemed so rude.
Shut it down? An unusual choice
Shut it down, but he heard the voice.

He heard the voice when he prayed.
He obeyed it and sent everyone away.
Hours later, the disaster came.
The warehouse close by burst into flames.

Flames consumed the port fast.
Soon after came the blast—
A massive explosion so loud,
Sending up a mushroom cloud.

Seconds after the blast gave,
A massive, giant shockwave.
Homes damaged as far as six miles.
For the Lebanese, a fiery trial.

Thousands injured, hundreds died.
The crater 400 feet wide.
But in the building of Life Center,
None had died who had entered.

The voice Pastor Deeb cherished,
If ignored, all would have perished.
He made the correct choice,
To listen to the Spirit's voice.

And when he held back none,
He activated, by faith, Psalm 91.

Inauguration Day

Parody of "Independence Day" by Martina McBride.

Well it seemed all right by dawn's early light;
Though, we all looked a little worried and weak.
I tried to pretend we weren't sinking again,
But then Pelosi got up to speak.

And I was only eight years old that summer.
President Reagan was leading the way,
And I think, now, of how far we have gone down
On Inauguration Day.

Well word gets around in a small, small town.
They said Biden was a dangerous man,
But Kamala was proud to run us into the ground.
But we knew they were not our friends.

Some cowards whispered, and some traitors talked.
But too many looked the other way.
And when Antifa came out, there was no one about
On Inauguration Day.

Let freedom ring. Let the righteous sing.
Let the whole world know that today,
The lies are deafening.
Let the weak be strong; don't let right be called wrong.
Let Hunter pay; don't throw that laptop away
On Inauguration Day.

Well the rioters lit up the sky like the Fourth of July.
By the time that the firemen came,
They just put out the flames
And took down some names
And just released them back to their homes.

Now no one makes clear what's right and what's wrong,
And as a nation, we have lost our way.
Talk about our constitution.
It's Inauguration Day.

Let freedom ring. Let the righteous sing.
Let the world know that today
There was election meddling.
Let the weak be strong; don't let right be called wrong.
Let Hunter pay; don't throw that laptop away
On Inauguration Day.

Pee Wee Sermon

I am resolved.
I am determined.
I'm done listening
To Pee Wee sermons.

Small substance,
Little impact,
Hard truth
These sermons subtract.

Sermons so soft;
Messages so sweet.
Void of protein.
Lacking meat.

No conviction,
They disappoint.
They fail continually
To get to the point.

They won't convict.
They won't offend,
So bring your family.
Bring your friends.

Soft sermons,
Skinny and lean.
Soft serve softer
Than Dairy Queen.

Entertaining and amusing
But not a life changer.
In the quiver, no arrows.
No warning of danger.

With every head bowed
And every eye closed,
Whole congregations
Asleep and dozed.

Now let me ask:
"Can you search?
Is Pee Wee Sermon
Preached at your church?"

Weary in the Waiting

Why do we worry
When God doesn't hurry
In our lives when we scurry?
Almighty God, miracles He can create,
But He gives us a word and then makes us wait.

There is a theory:
When life gets dreary
And we become weary,
He has not misled us in what we have heard,
But He causes us to go through the death of a word.

In that time of death,
When we can't feel His breath,
He's working a depth.
His promise to you may be delayed,
But He hasn't ignored you when you've prayed.

He builds our faith
When He hides His face,
And we can't sense His grace.
We can't be discouraged at any length.
Still the joy of the Lord is our strength.

In your waiting,
New things He's creating,
And your test He's grading.
He sees your heart and knows your desire.
He will walk with you right through the fire.

America the Dutiful

You should not question
Just submit and agree
Make no suggestion
From sea to shining sea

Do we remember
America the beautiful
Look at us now
America the dutiful

Following blindly
Makes our leaders proud
Voices have gone silent
Living to please the crowd

Do we remember
1776
But we'll build back better
Some echo voice predicts

Do as they say
But not as they do
And see the stars fade
On the red white and blue

America the dutiful
On a cliff so steep
America the dutiful
The bleating of the sheep

I Think We've All Known Now

Parody of "I Think We're Alone Now" by Tiffany.

"Children behave."
That's what Fauci says when we're together.
"And wash and obey.
Sanitize your hands."
And so we're

Masking just as fast as we can,
Not holding onto one another's hand,
Trying to get away into the night.
And he puts a second mask around me.
And I mumble out a sound, and then we say,

"I think we've all known, now,
How the Wuhan virus got spread around.
I think we've all known now.
Last year, the media made no sound."

Look at the way Fauci's gotta hide what he's doin'.
'Cause what would they say
If they ever knew? And so he's

Emailing just as fast as he can,
Standing in a pit of quick sand,
Trying to get away into the night.
And he puts a second mask around me.
And I mumble out a sound, and then we say,

"I think we've all known, now,
How the Wuhan virus got spread around.
I think we've all known now.
Finally, Fauci's lies are being found."

Led by Puppets

Land of puppets
Playing politicians
Behind the scenes.
Tricks by magicians.

Before our eyes,
Performing illusions.
Deception and lies,
Massive delusion.

Invisible strings
Pulled by their master,
Leading us faster
Toward disaster.

Puppets controlled
Behind the curtain.
Hidden agendas,
You can be certain.

Look behind the curtain.
Hidden puppeteers
Controlling politicians.
Transparency disappears.

Phony promises,
Fake smiles,
Bipartisan puppets
Both sides of the aisle.

Who controls
Who is speaking?
In this house of lies,
I hear some creaking.

Manipulating strings.
Making the simple believe.
Controlling minds.
Deceiving the naive.

Led by puppets
With strings attached.
From integrity,
They are detached.

Fire in the Snow

*David Brainerd was a missionary to the Indians in the 1700s.
He prayed so fervently that the heat from his body melted
the snow two feet around him. John Wesley said, "Let every
preacher read carefully the life of David Brainerd."*

In the woods burned a flame
A man prayed with urgency
He sought God earnestly
David Brainerd was his name

He took prayer to the next level
To the Spirit he had open ears
He did so much in a few years
He put fear in every devil

He prayed with passion in the snow
He long ago counted the cost
Over that ice there was a glow
Jesus saw his heart's desire

Through prayer he won the lost
In those woods burned a fire

Brace for Impact!

In our country today,
The foundation is cracked.
Time to get ready;
Brace for Impact!

We are at glide speed.
Loss of power we have felt.
Heads down! Stay down!
Fasten your seat belts.

We will be landing soon,
With no landing gear.
Prepare for a bumpy ride;
This landing is near.

Starting to nose dive,
No time for reflection.
Diving into the clouds
A year past the election.

Five hundred!
Fighting off fear.
Heads down! Stay down!
The ground is near.

One hundred!
Terrain, terrain! Pull up!
Mayday, Mayday!
Terrain, terrain! Pull up!

Fifty!
Wings begin to sway.

Forty!
Time is *now* to pray.

Thirty!
Will we land intact?

Twenty!
Brace for impact.

Ten!
About to hit the ground.
God we need you
Before the violent sound!

Brace! Brace
For your survival.
For out of this crash,
Will come a revival.

In our backslidden land,
To Jesus, we must cry,
Or to our land and future,
We will soon say goodbye.

Dumbing Down America

The remake of "America" by Neil Diamond.

Hard.
Our youth aren't working hard,
Staying on their phones
And not out in the yard.

Free.
They want everything free.
We say adios
To the American dream.

Unemployment never ends.
They're dumbing down America.
Never have to work again.
They're dumbing down America.

Home—unemployment makes them stay.
Oh, they're dismantling right today.
There's no welfare reform.
No welfare reform.

Home—a moratorium space.
Don't have to pay for their place.
Indeed the new norm.
Indeed the new norm.

Everywhere around the world,
They're dumbing down America.
Every time that flag is burned,
They're dumbing down America.
In their colleges, hear them share.

They're dumbing down America.
At their phones see them stare.
They're dumbing down America.
They're dumbing down America.
They're dumbing down America.
They're dumbing down America.
They're dumbing down America
Today, today, today, today, today.

My stimulus 'tis of thee.
(Today)
Sweet land of rioting.
(Today)
Of freebies I sing.
(Today)

A Dictator to You

*Sung by President Biden to the American people to the
tune of "Right Here Waiting" by Richard Marx.*

Oceans apart day after day,
And I slowly go insane.
Executive orders I do sign,
And I just can't use my brain.

Now I can tax whomever.
You can wear a mask forever.
Wherever you go,
Whatever you do,
I will be a dictator to you.
Whatever it takes,
Oh, I will be fake.
I will be a dictator to you.

I took for granted all the crimes
That I got away with somehow.
I create disaster. I make some tears,
But I can't hear you now.
Oh, can't you see it maybe?
I got people being lazy.

Wherever you go,
Whatever you do,
I will be a dictator to you.
Whatever it takes,
Oh, I will be fake.
I will be a dictator to you.

I wonder how we can survive
This collapse,
But in the end, if I'm with you,
We won't advance.

Oh, can't you see it maybe?
I think I'm going crazy.
Wherever you go,
Whatever you do,
I will be a dictator to you.
Whatever it takes,
Oh, I will be fake.
I will be a dictator to you.

Pregnant Man Emoji

Scrolling emoji as fast as I can,
I heard soon there will be a pregnant man.
Man, oh man, I'm not a fan.
Not a fan of the pregnant man.

No, no. I don't think it was clear.
Maybe that emoji drinks too much beer.
Did I really see that on my phone here?
Yes, pregnant man emoji are near.

So I thought: *Wow. What is coming next?*
When would I use this emoji in a text?
Oh, I know when using it would be best.
Maybe when I ate too much Tex-Mex.

Here we are in the battle of the bulge.
It seems this reasoning has some holes
From the natural way Apple pulls.
The obscure created from these lost souls

I will give you my opinion, for what it's worth.
In my beliefs, I stay grounded upon the earth.
Now, maybe I have not done enough research,
But I do not believe a man can give birth.

If I see a man with a belly swelling
And if I hear he is pregnant on Ellen,
I will just say, "The story is not gellin',
And under his shirt is a watermelon."

You can be mad at me and shout.
You can say I'm extreme and full of doubt.
But I have to question this and think about—
But I don't want to think about how that baby comes out.

When Samson Became a Nation

Turn with me, in those ancient pages,
To a story throughout the ages.
And in that inspired book,
Lies a story we can't overlook.

A few words about Samson I will give.
A story our nation seems to relive.
Around Samson, corrupt governments,
But Samson, with God, had a covenant.

Enemies fought but did not prevail.
Samson, through God's power, did avail.
Attacks against him were repeated.
Through God's power, he was not defeated.

But over time, he compromised,
Downward trend not realized.
In that time of political strife,
Samson lived a double life.

Over time, he was no longer devout,
And Samson's eyes were plucked out.
Forgetting God was his poor decision,
Costing Samson his divine vision.

Where did losing his vision begin?
It began when Samson gave in to sin.
America, like Samson, has lost her vision,
Forsaking God—our Samson decision.

Samson, Samson, where is your strength?
Have you forgotten your hair and its length?
Samson nation have you cut your hair?
Has your strength vanished unaware?

The warning signs couldn't be any plainer:
Lost his hair and became an entertainer.
America resembles Samson in this hour,
Forgetting the source of our power.

America will be humbled to her knees.
We will find God in hardship, not in ease.
But Samson looked up at the very end.
His heart was humbled and did bend.

We can't control the future and beyond,
But still to a Samson nation, God will respond.
So grab the pillars and begin to pray,
And God will remember our country today.

We Built Self Pity

The remake of "We Built This City" by Starship.

We built self-pity.
We built self-pity on young and old.
Built self-pity.
We built self-pity on young and old.

Say you don't work, see. Stay in your safe place.
Say you don't care with a pout upon your face.
How low will they stoop, yeah, giving up the fight?
Too many pandering and thinking it's alright.

Free ponies and their momma. Give them some Play-Doh. Don't you remember?
We built self-pity. We built self-pity on young and old.

We built self-pity.
We built self-pity on young and old.
Built self-pity.
We built self-pity on young and old.

Someone's always playing inflation games.
Who cares? They're always changing taxation names.
It feels like France here; hear the voices rage.
I call them irresponsible, wanting a free wage.

Free ponies and their momma. Give them some Play-Doh. Don't you remember?
We built self-pity. We built self-pity on young and old.

We built self-pity.
We built self-pity on young and old.
Built self-pity.
We built self-pity on young and old.

Who thinks it's funny, lowering the bar?
Who took their brains and put them into jars?
Don't tell them you need them 'cause they're the ship of fools
Looking at our leaders indoctrinate our schools.

Free ponies and their momma. Give them some Play-Doh. Don't you remember?
We self-pity. We built self-pity on young and old.

We built self-pity.
We built self-pity on young and old.
Built self-pity.
We built self-pity on young and old.

Press One for English

Press one for English
Press two for Español
Press three for French
Press five if you don't know

Press eight for Italian
And one if you are in a rig
Press one one more time
Before you try to dig

Press six for domestic
Press one to go global
Press one one more time
To speak to T-Mobile

Then stay on hold
Be transferred again
Then get disconnected
That's where you begin

Press one again for English
Press two for Español
Press zero over and over
If you are vexed in your soul

Prepare Him Room

Come with me to the Bethlehem Inn,
To a motel with no room for Him.
No one was aware.
Inside, they were sleeping.
No one was searching.
No one was seeking.

A world of darkness,
A world of fear,
But no one knew the Savior was here.
Before there was an empty tomb,
There was a motel with no room.

Darkness prevails today,
Or so it seems.
Evil exalted to the extremes.
Jesus still lives in spite of the gloom,
But yet men still have no room.

Room for themselves,
Room for pleasure,
But no room for the greatest treasure.
They ignore Him in the silent night,
Rejecting the brightness of His light.

Locate the star.
Come and rejoice.
Choose today to make the choice.
Life will go on, I presume.
But will you choose to prepare Him room?

Not For Me but for Thee

In the words of our politicians.

Not for me but for thee.
Not for thee to be free,
But it's for me to decree.
Controlling you is key.
Restrictions you can guarantee,
But not for me but for thee.

You can argue and disagree
While we sip and drink our tea.
Complain and press your plea.
From our standard, we will flee.
Who made you referee?
Not for me but for thee.

I'm about me and not about we.
To break my rules, I am free.
Hypocrisy deep as the sea,
Yet I ignore you with glee.
I don't care if you disagree.
Not for me but for thee.

I cover my ears to your plea
And to the kids who are not free.
I care about health you see.
Actually no, I care about me.
I just pretend and let it be.
Not for me but for thee.

I'm posturing like a tree
Along with many celebrities.
Hear the saying: When you see
Politicians of three, let them be.
I refuse to walk the talk, you see.
Not for me but for thee.

You Don't Have to Be a Prophet

You don't have to be a prophet
You don't have to have a vision
To know we are so blinded
With all of our division

You don't have to be a prophet
You don't have to dream dreams
To see this instability
Tearing at the seams

You don't have to be a prophet
To hear the prophetic sound
When we see our colleges
And our youth they are dumbing down

You don't have to be a prophet
You could have just guessed
We are about to see more riots
Heading toward more unrest

You don't have to be a prophet
To gaze into the future
To know we are in trouble
In our blinded stupor

You don't have to be a prophet
You can see it all around
The love of most grows cold
And lawlessness abounds

You don't have to be a prophet
To see we've built with stubble
Or to see America's future
Will be through days of trouble

You don't have to be a prophet
To see prayer is what we need
And without the hand of God
Our nation will not succeed

You don't have to be a prophet
To wait and take action
You don't have to be a prophet
To pray with faith and passion

Trolls of the Underground

There once was an internet troll
Who drank Kool-Aid by the bowl.
Gave a hearty amen
To all on CNN,
The talking points he stole.

Here comes the internet troll.
With a hidden profile, he does roll.
Online he feels empowered
But truly just a coward.
We wonder if he has a soul.

No reasoning with the trolls,
I guess that's their goal.
They just play the game
With some imaginary name.
Of hate and anger, they are full.

Who are these internet trolls?
Are they shopping down at Kohl's?
Oh, where do they roam?
Are they gaming at home?
Do their parents pay their bills in full?

On social media, if you stroll,
It's easy to find these trolls.
Online they are cursing
But so timid in person,
Staying underground in their holes.

A Trip to Moses Lake, Washington

I went to a place called Moses Lake
To go out to eat and have a steak,
But the steakhouse was closed.
So I took the mask off my nose.
Instead, I just went out to the lake.

Someone in the lake took a bath.
Over their nose, they still wore a mask.
It felt nice when it got hotter,
But I couldn't part the waters.
Of course, I didn't have Moses's staff.

I saw masks up high when outside.
I thought, at me, others would chide.
So I got down on my hands
And sneezed in the sand
Then built a sand castle two feet high.

I decided to mosey on down the road
Before my rental car got towed.
I grabbed my potato chips
And left this mask apocalypse,
Headed toward Idaho and my abode.

In Idaho, people were still free.
No one gave dirty looks at me.
I hope they stay in the battle
And don't end up like Seattle.
So I can still vacation there you see.

Walk Like a Politician

Remake of "Walk like an Egyptian" by the Bangles.

All the leaders in the backroom,
They do the same dance. Don't you know?
With all their tricks (oh whey oh),
Most should be in Guantanamo.

The blind line up in single file
While they keep playing the great reset.
Leftist crocodiles (oh whey oh),
They snap their teeth on the internet.

Foreign types block our rights, say.
(Whey oh. Whey oh. Ay. Oh whey oh.)
"Walk like a politician."

The blind lead the blind today.
They spin around, and you they ignore.
They disapprove (oh whey oh).
They drop one lie, and then they drop ten more.

All the school kids brainwashed books.
Now conservatives are being banned.
When big brother sings, (oh whey oh)
They walk like a politician.

All the kids in the workplace say,
(Whey oh. Whey oh. Ay. Oh whey oh.)
"Walk like a politician."

On freedom, there's an all-out attack
Being led by a bunch of quacks.
Truth they change, you know (oh whey oh)
While they drive their Cadillacs.

They wanna defund all the cops.
They won't be hanging out in the donut shops.
They sing and dance (oh whey oh).
They help the rioters down the block.

Do you hear their rhetoric again?
The White House becomes the Kremlin,
And the Chinese know (oh whey oh).
They walk over our politicians.

And all the cops they try to block say,
(Whey oh. Whey oh. Ay. Oh whey oh.)
"Walk like a politician.
Walk like a politician."

The Evan-Jelly-Full Church

In the church as a whole,
We've become evan jelly full.
Sweet treats we do provide:
Doughnuts with jelly inside.

Preached sermons incomplete,
Full of sugar and little meat.
No conviction the message brings,
Leaving out the harder things.

To encourage and to inspire
But on the altar, no fire.
Light topics we like covering,
But avoid the call of suffering.

Sin is mentioned but not specific.
Eternal results are not terrific.
Content with this beautiful façade,
But yet we lack the fear of God.

Messages spoken so gently.
Services so seeker friendly.
God's Presence we can't expect
When we've become politically correct.

Why is the message so soft we bring?
Are we just concerned about offerings?
Bright lights and fog machines,
But where is God on the scene?

Are doughnuts the church's mission?
With jelly inside and no nutrition?
The evan-jelly-full church is the new norm.
Not hold or cold but only lukewarm.

The Chihuahua from Chicago

There was a Chihuahua from Chicago—
A friendly dog but tough, you know.
He would be courteous and polite,
But if you crossed him, he'd bite.
His street name was Santiago.

He hung out by West Garfield Park.
It was hard to hear him when he would bark.
At nighttime, in certain spots,
All you would hear was gunshots.
It happened every evening after dark.

There was crime all over those streets.
Nobody was handing out doggy treats.
This was by no means a resort
North of the Midway airport,
And over and over crime repeats.

The city was bad, and things got nutty.
But he still hung out with his buddies.
They would go out for pita
Or to meet senoritas.
Once in a while run around and get muddy.

There was graffiti from paint sprayers.
Santiago's head needed some Bayer.
Problems seemingly insurmountable,
No one ever held them accountable.
Nothing was ever done by the mayor.

The mayor helped to defund the police.
In Chicago, it's catch and release.
So bad guys keep on shooting,
And criminals keep on looting.
For Santiago, there was no peace.

One day, an idea came to Santiago.
He got online and checked out Trivago.
He booked himself a trip
On a huge cruise ship.
For once, he got himself out of Chicago.

For a week, he enjoyed his getaway.
In the windy city, he didn't want to stay.
So when he got his diploma,
He moved to Oklahoma.
To him, that was the most glorious day.

He still FaceTimed his buddies on his phone.
He'd send them a care package with a bone.
But he had no regrets he left,
Not missing the murder and theft,
Relieved to be out of that war zone.

He missed hanging out with his friend Diego,
But staying in Chicago was *no bueno*.
He sure was glad to be gone
From where guns were always drawn.
He was willing to take a risk on a tornado.

Ice on Your Wings

Have you gotten cold,
Distracted by other things?
Are you weighed down
By ice on your wings?

It can seem minor.
It can appear small.
But just a little ice
Can cause you to stall.

Have you checked your heart?
Does it need to melt?
Or is it too hard
For the Spirit to be felt?

There's coming a change.
There will soon be a shift.
You were created for flight.
You were destined for lift.

So deice your wings,
And press in and pray.
Departure time is here.
Head for the runway.

You're cleared for takeoff.
Time to add full power.
Will you crash or soar
In this crucial hour?

Feet Cross the Line

The remake of "Sweet Caroline" by Neil Diamond.

When it began,
I think we all kind of know.
But now they are coming in strong
Came in the spring,
And the spring became summer.
Who'd have believed they'd all come along?

Handouts from our hands.
Illegals out, costing me. Costing you.

Feet cross the line.
Good has now been withstood.
Our leaders have been inclined
To not visit like they should.
But now I

Look at the line, and it doesn't seem so lonely.
They filled it with a million too.
And when they vote,
Voting left is what they're told there.
How can I vote when they're voting too?

One robbing one.
Illegals out, costing me. Costing you.

Feet cross the line.
Good has now been withstood.
Our leaders have been inclined
To not visit like they should.
Oh no. No.

Feet cross the line.
Good has now been withstood.
Feet cross the line.
I believed they always could.
Feet cross the line.
Good has now been withstood.

Your Wilderness Will Soon End

Your wilderness will soon end
In your dry and barren land
Deliverance God will send

He hasn't forgotten you my friend
He still has you by His hand
Your wilderness will soon end

Though struggles seem to extend
And trials we don't understand
Deliverance God will send

His ear to you He will bend
Through a way you have not planned
Your wilderness will soon end

From the valley you will ascend
Hardship you will withstand
Deliverance God will send

You will see miracles firsthand
Your vision He will expand
Your wilderness will soon end
Deliverance God will send

America, Come Back to Thee

As the frightening storm nears,
People continue to cover their ears.
Observe the unrest, and discern the fears.

Striving goes on, and wars don't cease.
Yet some men think it will decrease,
Saying, "Peace. Peace when there is no peace."

The naive live their lives, ignoring
The truth. They go on scorning,
Foolishly neglecting the warning.

I can't hear the warning cry,
But I can see the blackened sky.
Does anyone have a prophetic eye?

Can America still be sustained
When a twisted reality is explained?
When men only want to be entertained?

The ignorant go on living their lives
While politicians throw their knives.
In this storm blackout, who survives?

Empty activity numbs and distracts,
But still our nation has gone off the tracks.
In our foundation, notice the cracks.

Hence the sky calmly begins to rain.
An hour of trial and an hour of pain.
But our righteousness we will regain.

America, America—land of the free.
Jesus cries out to us, you see.
America, America. Come back to thee!

Miracle in the Deep

*The story of Robert Gause, this poem is dedicated to
all the brave men of the USS Indianapolis.*

On July 30, 1945,
The USS *Indianapolis* did not arrive,
But there's something we can glean.
From one of the 317
Shows us that God is still alive.

The story is about Robert Gause
On the ship that suffered loss.
In water for five days,
But he still gave God praise.
In his test, he clung to the cross.

All prayed and raised a sound,
But Gause thanked God they would be found.
His was faith was great,
Though God seemed late.
He believed and did not drown.

Sun scorched by day, freezing at dark.
Others didn't make it, eaten by sharks.
Spotting planes was key,
But never seen in the sea.
Hopelessness leaving its mark.

Before this struggle in the Pacific,
Gause learned to make his prayers specific.
He saw God, in the past,
Respond to what he asked.
God showed up in the horrific.

In breaking up a fight, he did his best,
But salt water he did ingest.
From the group, he did drift.
Looked like death would be swift,
But God appeared in his test.

Beginning to lose his mind,
He sought God and did find.
Before life was blackened,
A divine miracle happened.
His death sentence was declined.

God saw Robert's prayer and devotion.
His feet somehow rested on the floor of the ocean.
He rested for hours.
God showed His power,
Set a miracle for Gause in motion.

He had no more strength to swim,
But the ocean floor came up to meet him.
God heard Robert's heart
In the ocean's deepest part,
In despair when all looked grim.

From this story, what can we glean
From Gause and the 317?
In our darkest hour,
Trust in God's power,
And God will show up on the scene.

For Such a Time as This

Written in the summer of 2020 during the riots of our major cities.

In this time of chaos,
One thing you cannot miss.
You are the light in the darkness
For such a time as this.

Our nation has turned to violence.
The riots are appalling.
But for such a time as this,
You will enter into your calling.

It's not by accident you are here.
God has prepared you for this day.
Many miracles will happen
For those that will believe and pray.

From Portland to Indy,
From Spokane to Detroit,
God's people will be strong
And do mighty exploits.

Without God on this ship,
We would have no sail.
For such a time as this,
We will be strong and not fail.

In these difficult times,
Hamans have arisen,
But they cannot stop
The divine appointed vision.

Trampling on what is right,
Evil seems to fester.
But in this hour,
God still has an Esther.

For the Jews long ago,
The end was near.
But Queen Esther chose
To not walk in fear.

For such a time as this,
Esther's spirit woke.
Her words brought change
To the nation when she spoke.

Haman is here,
But the Esther company will arise
To speak the truth
And not compromise.

So in this chaotic time,
It's not all happiness and bliss.
But know you are here
For such a time as this.